D1522431

A Strategy for Stable Peace

A Strategy for Stable Peace
Toward a Euroatlantic Security Community

James E. Goodby
Petrus Buwalda
Dmitri Trenin

UNITED STATES INSTITUTE OF PEACE PRESS
Washington, D.C.

ASSOCIATION FOR DIPLOMATIC STUDIES AND TRAINING
Arlington, Virginia

355.033018
G64N

The views expressed in this book are those of the authors alone. They do not necessarily reflect views of the United States Institute of Peace or the Association for Diplomatic Studies and Training.

UNITED STATES INSTITUTE OF PEACE
1200 17th Street NW, Suite 200
Washington, DC 20036-3011

ASSOCIATION FOR DIPLOMATIC STUDIES
AND TRAINING
4000 Arlington Boulevard
Arlington, VA 22204-1586

First published 2002

Printed in the United States of America

The paper used in this publication meets the minimum requirements of American National Standards for Information Science—Permanence of Paper for Printed Library Materials, ANSI Z39.48-1984.

Library of Congress Cataloging-in-Publication Data
Goodby, James E.
    A strategy for stable peace : toward a Euroatlantic security community /
James E. Goodby, Petrus Buwalda, Dmitri Trenin
      p. cm.
    Includes bibliographical references and index.
    ISBN 1-929223-32-3
    1. National security—Europe. 2. National security—United States.
3. National security—Russia (Federation) 4. World politics—21st century. 5. European Union—Defenses. 6. United States—Defenses. 7. Russia (Federation)—Defenses. I. Buwalda, Piet, 1925– II. Trenin, Dmitri.
III. Title

UA646.G587 2001
355'.03301821—dc21
                                   2001039786

For Alexander George—J. E. G.

For my grandsons, Daniel and Julius—P. B.

For Yury Davidov—D. V. T.

Contents

Preface

T HE DEVASTATING TERRORIST ATTACKS on the World Trade Center in New York City and on the Pentagon near Washington, D.C., in September 2001 elicited a tremendous feeling of solidarity between Europe and North America. The unanimous acceptance of the application of Article 5 of the North Atlantic Treaty (an attack on one is an attack on all) both by the old allies and by those countries that had recently joined NATO, was much more than a public relations exercise. Every ally realized what was involved and none took the decision lightly. The European Union stated its full support shortly afterward.

For its part, Russia has declared itself an ally of the West. In doing so, Putin and his associates have made a strategic choice rather than a tactical move. Beyond the prospects for practical cooperation in the fight against international terrorism, broader vistas open. The Russian leadership has concluded that the situation is propitious for making strides toward Russia's integration into Western political, economic, and military structures on mutually acceptable terms. This gives America and Western Europe a rare chance to solve the "Russia problem" in a constructive and conclusive way. This also gives Russia a chance to establish a new international identity. Russia's integration would be similar in kind, although not in manner, to the successful integration of Germany and Japan after World War II, and would open the way to expanding the community of countries enjoying stable peace in their mutual relations throughout the Euroatlantic area.

Long-term vision and concrete action are both needed if this integration is to take place; common values must be reaffirmed while action is taken to deal with a plethora of practical issues rooted in national interests. Building support for Russia's integration with the West will require concerted action at different levels in America, in Europe, and in Russia itself. Although the integration process will inevitably proceed step by step and stage by stage, the final objective should be clear from the outset: Russia as a European country in every respect, including its membership of Western institutions. The stakes are high, but so are the expected benefits. If this opportunity is missed, the challenge to civilization that appeared so tragically on September 11, 2001, will not have been matched with the response that it deserves, and other goals shared by Russia and the West will be more difficult to achieve.

The manuscript for this book was completed before September 11. However, even before the attacks on New York and Washington, we had concluded that joint and parallel actions to achieve a stable peace within the Euroatlantic community would strengthen our nations' ability to make war on terrorism as well as to deal with other global challenges. Assessments of the meaning of the events of September 11 have only underscored that judgment.

The latest crisis has shown once more that constant consultation and communication among us is indispensable. No nation can go it alone nor can any democratic government afford to be drawn into struggles about which it is insufficiently informed or in which it has no say over the means to be employed.

The construction of a stable peace within the Euroatlantic community of nations will not require the destruction of those special characteristics that have made our nations so distinct. What will be different is that war among them will become a part of history, not a part of their panoply of policy options. To accomplish this, all of the nations involved must recognize that they are alike more than they are different. They must see themselves as the builders of a common community, and they must be determined to translate this vision into reality.

This book results from the experiences and reflections of its three authors. It is a jointly written book in the sense that we exchanged drafts, consulted together in person and via e-mail, and freely gave and accepted suggestions and critiques. However, Trenin took the lead in drafting chapter 2, Buwalda in drafting chapter 3, and Goodby in drafting the introduction, chapter 1, and chapter 4. We wrote chapters 5 and 6 together.

A book that sets out to show how a stable peace could be achieved between Russia and the West, we believed, should be a shared effort of an American, a Western European, and a Russian. This book has benefited from the differing perspectives and career experiences we brought to bear on the analysis. We do not want to suggest that our thinking is in the exact center of political thought in the European Union, Russia, or the United States. But we are hardheaded observers of the scene we wanted to describe and have few illusions about the world we live in. We think that our analysis and our recommendations are realistic, that is, well within the political limits all national leaders must live within. We have further benefited from the insights and judgments of Yves Pagniez, former ambassador of France in Moscow and Belgrade and senior policymaker in the Quai d'Orsay. A commentary by Ambassador Pagniez on the European Union appears after chapter 3.

We owe a debt of thanks to the United States Institute of Peace for sponsoring the study from which this book was derived, and to the Association for Diplomatic Studies and Training, which was the financial manager of a grant generously provided by the Institute to defray the expenses of research and writing. In 1998 the Institute published a book by James Goodby entitled *Europe Undivided,* which dealt with the concept of an inclusive Euroatlantic security community that would achieve stable peace. Acting on the advice of Ambassador Max Kampelman, Richard Solomon, president of the Institute, then directed that a Future of Europe Working Group be established to map out

more specifically how, step-by-step, a peaceful, undivided, and democratic Europe could be achieved. Anthony Lake, former U.S. national
security adviser to President Clinton, and Stephen Hadley, now U.S.
deputy national security adviser to President George W. Bush, agreed
to cochair the working group.

From the beginning of the project in 1998 through 2000, the Future
of Europe Working Group met regularly under cochairs Hadley and
Lake. As project director, Goodby generally participated, as did Institute director of Research and Studies Patrick Cronin, program officer
Lauren Van Metre, and, later, program officer Emily Metzgar. Goodby
thanks the members of the Future of Europe Working Group and its
cochairmen for their ideas and insights, many of which have found
their way into this book.

The Institute cosponsored three international conferences to
bring together Americans and Europeans for the purpose of considering the feasibility and desirability of a peaceful, undivided, and democratic Europe and how such a Europe might some day come to pass.
The first was held at the U.S. Foreign Service Institute in Arlington,
Virginia, in October 1998. The second was at the Aspen Institute, Berlin,
in January 2000 and the third was at the Royal Institute of International Affairs (Chatham House), London, in October 2000. These three
institutes generously joined with the United States Institute of Peace
in sponsoring the conferences at their respective headquarters. Each
of the three authors participated in one or more of the international
conferences.

We benefited significantly from the advice given to us in reviews
arranged by the United States Institute of Peace. Our editor, Dr. Nigel
Quinney, was our constant companion during the last stages of writing
this book. We are deeply indebted to the Institute for making a person of his rare talents available to us. President Richard Solomon and
Dr. Patrick Cronin were steady supporters of this study throughout,
as was Mr. Dan Snodderly, director of Publications. Their firm belief
in the utility of taking a long view made them rare, if not unique, persons in the policy community.

Readers can perhaps imagine the challenges of communicating
regularly between Washington, The Hague, Moscow, and Paris in the

process of exchanging drafts and redrafts of the manuscript for this book. The person who took on much of the responsibility for this was Priscilla Goodby. The authors are deeply grateful to her for her dedication and skill in keeping us all moving harmoniously toward that goal.

Finally, we venture the opinion that the present decade is one of the turning points of history. Other turning points have ended in tragedies for humankind. This one may be different. We can only hope that the tragedy of September 11, 2001, will help to make it so. Relations between the nations of the Euroatlantic community have changed in fundamental ways and this is probably irreversible. Globalization and technology are remaking the international environment. The idea that war can be a rational way to resolve problems between major nations, if not discredited altogether, has very few adherents—none that we know of in positions of high responsibility in governments within the Euroatlantic community. Our sense is that if leaders are guided by the instincts of their people they will look to the future, to the stable peace that is theirs to win, and to the immense good that their community can do in the world. The next few years will be decisive.

JAMES E. GOODBY   PETRUS BUWALDA   DMITRI TRENIN
WASHINGTON, D.C.   THE HAGUE   MOSCOW

A Strategy for Stable Peace

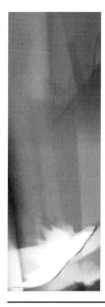

Introduction

THE UNITED STATES AND RUSSIA AND ALL THE NATIONS OF EUROPE can eliminate war as a means of settling disputes among themselves. It will not be easy but it is within their reach and it would have enormous global consequences—all good. We explain our reasoning in the chapters that follow and propose practical policies that will move the nations toward a stable peace. We present perspectives on a stable peace from the vantage point of Russia, the United States, and Western Europe.

Throughout our discussion, we use a few shorthand terms to describe our thinking. The nations of North America and Europe, including Russia, can collectively be described as a *system,* because of the powerful reciprocal influences they exert upon one another. Because of their geography, history, and culture, this set of nations can be called an *extended European system.* In parts of the system, particularly North America, Western Europe, and Northwestern Europe, war has been excluded as a policy option: peace has become *stable.* We assume that a Europe that is *peaceful, undivided, and democratic,* a phrase often used by former U.S. president Bill Clinton, is a close approximation of a system of nations under stable peace and therefore use the term "stable peace" in that sense. Former president George

3

Bush and President George W. Bush have invoked the vision of a "Europe whole and free," evidently to convey the same idea. Neither "undivided" nor "whole" implies homogeneity, only that transactions within the system do not make distinctions based on ideology, cultural differences, or military relations. The idea of diversity within a unifying framework was stressed by President George W. Bush when he spoke of "a Europe that is truly united, truly democratic and truly diverse, a collection of peoples and nations bound together in purpose and respect, and faithful to their own roots."[1]

In some parts of Europe, as in the Balkans, peace may still be *precarious;* war could be just around the corner. In most of the system, especially between Russia and the West, war has not yet been excluded and military deterrence remains a factor in interstate relations, even though war is a remote contingency. This situation can be called a *conditional* peace.[2] The question this book addresses is whether a stable peace could be extended beyond its present beachhead to include all, or nearly all, of the nations within the extended European system.

There is such a thing as a "just war." Wars to resist tyrannies and to stop genocide are in this category. When we write about stable peace in Europe it is essential for our readers to understand that we are not implying the triumph of pacifism. Nor are we thinking of a peace imposed by a dominant imperial power. Rather, we are visualizing a peace in which no state within a given system of states ever considers the use of military options against another state within the system to pursue or safeguard its interests, or even considers using threats of force in any dispute between them. Deterrence and compellance strategies backed by military force are excluded as instruments of policy within the system. Such strategies may very well be commonplace as instruments of policy when states deal with threats that arise outside the system. Serious disputes may occur within the system but they are dealt with by nonmilitary instruments of policy. Examples where stable peace has been achieved include the European Union and U.S. relations with Western European nations, Canada, and Mexico. Chapter 1 discusses how such circumstances may arise.

A stable peace of this sort within the extended European system would be far preferable to the historical norm, where wars within the system have occurred regularly, interspersed with frequent war-threatening crises. Aside from releasing the members of the system for more productive internal activities, the absence of war within the system eliminates one key source of global armed conflict. An additional advantage would accrue to these nations if the absence of war made it possible for them to act harmoniously within the extended European system and with some coherence in global affairs.

The chances of Europe enjoying a stable peace may seem remote, but the reunification of Germany also seemed to be a dream until it happened. A stable peace throughout Europe is a serious strategic objective, well within the realm of reality. It is a practical and realizable goal that deserves concentrated and high-level attention. This goal must be explicitly identified as the central purpose of the nations within the extended European system and of plans prepared to achieve it. Key to a stable peace, inevitably, are those policies that will shape the relationships among the nations of the European Union, Russia, and the United States and this is what we discuss in this book.

The idea of a stable peace is closely related to another concept, that of a *security community*—another idea we use in our analysis. As defined by the U.S. scholar Karl Deutsch and others, a security community is a group of nations within which "there is real assurance that the members of that community will not fight each other physically, but will settle their disputes in some other way." We postulate that a security community is a rudimentary form of a stable peace. In this stage of development, we imagine that the differences, especially in value systems, between states within a security community would be more pronounced than in a system of nations that had achieved a stable peace.[3]

Many desirable attributes of a stable peace could be achieved among states whose values, forms of government, and economies differ in important respects. However, security communities may more easily disintegrate precisely because of their underlying differences. Therefore, we think that a stable peace is the right ultimate goal for the nations to pursue. The process of getting to a stable peace may be about the same as the process of getting to a security community. In the early stages, in particular, strategies aimed at moving beyond a conditional peace would be the same, whether the nations think of themselves as working toward a security community or a true stable peace.

Treating a stable peace as a proposition meant to be taken seriously by governments is a good disciplinary framework for considering the future course of relations within an extended European system of nations. The euphoria of the early 1990s has given way to a more sober view of international relationships, but the present decade still is a hinge point in history, a time when relationships can be influenced in one direction or another. If ever there was a time for long-term analysis and strategic thinking, this is it. The upheavals associated with the end of the Cold War, for better or worse, have not yet given way to a settled international order. Closer cooperation between the European Union, Russia, and the United States could create a powerful and positive nucleus for the developing international order. This is what President George W. Bush endorsed as his own commitment: "A Europe and an America bound in a great alliance of liberty, history's greatest united force for peace and progress and human dignity."[4]

Only if governments have a clearer idea than they currently seem to have of where they would like European relations to be in ten or twenty years will it be possible to devise complementary strategies and plans to carry them out. This is easier said than done, for several very big and relevant questions will be answered only over the course of time. But governments can shape the answers to these questions, and their duty is to do so with a keen awareness of the stakes involved:

❖ Will the United States remain a major actor on the European scene or will economic and demographic factors lead it to focus its energies elsewhere?

❖ What are the prospects for Russia's seeing itself—and for others seeing Russia—as a "normal" member of an extended European system?

❖ Will the necessary overhaul of the European Union's decision-making process occur in time to permit the rapid and orderly expansion of the European Union to the east? How will the different rates of adaptation to technology and globalization affect the prospects for an extended European system that is peaceful, undivided, and democratic?

❖ How might Asian power centers (China, Korea, Japan, India) relate to an extended European security community?

❖ Can Euroatlantic institutions evolve to support a security community centered on Europe that includes the United States and Russia?

These questions all fall into the category of imponderables at the moment, but this does not excuse governments from considering how the answers would advance the extended European system beyond its present state of conditional peace. We offer our opinions on many of these questions as a way of stimulating debate. After centuries of war in Europe, and with images of the latest ones still fresh, a stable peace may seem illusory. But we think that enough has changed in Europe and in the world—not least the fact that this kind of peace has materialized in places—to make the idea a practical one, one worthy of a central place in national strategic thinking. For the first time in history, it is worth remembering, the United States and Russia are both engaged in creating institutions that will link North America and *all* the states of Europe. The French financial expert and adviser to post–World War II French governments, Jean Monnet, conceived the idea of French-German reconciliation through economic cooperation and integration. Eventually, this idea led to a European Union that really is something new under the sun. Franco-German rapprochement teaches us that states with major cultural and political differences can move toward harmonious relations, building on issues of practical interest.

To begin the analysis of this proposition, we suggest in chapter 1 that underlying social and other factors within each nation will dictate whether a stable peace can be achieved. In common with many scholars and political figures, we assume that democratic values and a shared sense of identity are among the most important of these preconditions and we are optimistic that this requirement will be met. That said, we stress that concerted national strategies on the part of the major nations within the extended European system are essential for progress toward a stable peace. Without concerted policies, neither globalization nor favorable internal developments will suffice to achieve a stable peace. The disruptive effects of residual adversarial attitudes within the system, and of quarrels injected into it from regional conflicts around its periphery, will hamper the consolidation of common value systems and cooperative practices. The major actors must consciously adopt policies aimed at overcoming these disruptive effects. Also in chapter 1 we suggest various structural forms that a security community centered on Europe might assume and conclude that the form most conducive to a stable peace would be a triad in which the main centers of gravity are the European Union, Russia, and the United States, with no one of them dominant. This structure is very different from the bipolar order of the Cold War period and, of course, also different from the benign American hegemony advocated by some and opposed by others.

Chapters 2–4 present perspectives from Russia, the European Union, and the United States. Each author is convinced that stable peace in Europe is a feasible and highly desirable goal. From a Russian perspective, presented in chapter 2, it appears that differences between Russia and the West are not fundamental. Partnership with the European Union and cooperative relations with the Atlantic Alliance would improve Russia's security situation. In the long run, the development in Russia of a civil society based on democratic principles will be necessary to establish qualitatively new links between Russia and the West.

From a Western European perspective, presented in chapter 3, the European Union has consolidated a stable peace in the western part of the continent. Now the Union is at a critical juncture. Can it make the leap forward in its internal structure that will be necessary to deal with expansion to the east without losing its cohesion as a community of values and pooled sovereignties? If the Union accepts new members in 2004 while avoiding significant internal reform, its contribution to a stable peace will be diminished. Thus the historic achievement of a stable peace through the efforts of the nations of the European Union depends heavily on the courage and vision of national leadership in Western Europe in the next two to three years. The external policies of the Union toward Russia and the United States also are important, especially in fostering partnerships among all three parties; these policies could be focused more sharply than they are on a strategy for a stable peace.

Ambassador Yves Pagniez, writing from the perspective of long service as a French diplomat, offers his reflections on several of these issues in a commentary following chapter 3. He reminds us that common foreign policies still leave room for national differences and that this can foster innovation. His view of the European Union's role in Europe and the world underscores the Union's autonomy in a tripolar relationship with Russia and the United States. In harmony with the three authors, Ambassador Pagniez stresses the importance of democratic developments in Russia for a stable peace.

Chapter 4 provides a U.S. perspective, noting that U.S. public opinion is favorably inclined toward the kinds of cooperative policies necessary to promote a stable peace. This chapter argues that a security community centered on Europe is feasible because of historic and cultural ties and because of developments since World War II that may make it possible to overcome the divisions and hostilities of the past.

Broad cultural, geopolitical, regional, demographic, economic, and technological developments, some beyond the reach of governments, will affect the course of events. Nevertheless, governments can influence decisively the prospects for a Europe that is peaceful, undivided, and democratic. To do so, they must align national policies with fundamental trends in human affairs or must try to influence those trends that can be nudged one way or another. In chapter 5, taking account of attitudes within the European Union, Russia, and the United States, we seek to define parallel and complementary policies that, together, would constitute a coordinated strategy for a stable peace. These policies, including internal actions, are directed at building sustainable ties that will have some growth potential. We do not believe that a detailed "master plan" to achieve a stable peace is realistic. Rather, governments should work with building blocks already available to them, having their objective clearly in mind.[5]

Short- or mid-term initiatives that will serve long-term ends are proposed in chapter 6. They include cooperation in ballistic missile defense, export controls, preventive diplomacy to avoid regional conflicts, trade and financial dealings, and a series of proposals designed to engage a broad range of people directly in cooperative activities. Our purpose here is to set out an array of ideas that are responsive to current needs as we see them. Working together within the framework afforded by this pattern of cooperation will set the members of the extended European system firmly on the road to a stable peace.

The use or threat of military force in post–Cold War Europe has not been abolished. That has been established by several precedents, and these experiences have played a part in defining the community that will evolve in Europe. Whether the nations have intended it or not, these actions—and sometimes inactions—are creating a body of norms and expected rules of behavior. But are the norms and rules uniform throughout the whole system of nations? Experiences in the Balkans and in the North Caucasus illustrate the problems that arise when principles of international law are in conflict, as they were in the cases of Kosovo and Chechnya, where sovereignty and nonintervention in internal affairs came into conflict with human rights. In Yugoslavia the principle of nonintervention was sacrificed to reverse a massive violation of human rights; in Russia, a Chechen challenge to Russia's sovereignty was defeated by methods that violated basic norms of human rights. In both cases, military solutions were imposed instead of political solutions, which would have been preferable, setting precedents that will have long-term repercussions (and that have already had damaging short-term effects). These experiences have opened a breach between Russia and the West. Unless it can be repaired, not only will norms and rules be different in different parts of Europe, but the idea of a stable peace will face further obstacles. More than a decade after the end of the Cold War, a gulf still exists between Russia and the West, and Europe is only conditionally at peace, a situation that must not be allowed to continue, not least because the struggle against a common enemy—terrorism—requires the unity of the Euroatlantic community.

1

The Outlook for a Stable Peace

THE CAUSES OF PEACE

How does a stable peace develop between two or more states? The explanations are diverse, and debatable. The fundamental requirement very likely is a common value system—almost certainly democratic values. And this raises the question of Russia's future: can Russia's current institutions of government evolve into a sturdy and settled mode of democratic governance? Of course, Russian democratic values and democratic governance should not be expected to manifest themselves in exactly the same form as those of the United States or of any other existing democracy. Cultural factors and historical experiences dictate the particular form in which democratic values are expressed.

Since there is no settled theory as to the causes of a stable peace, we should point out that stable peace might be achieved in ways other than through democratic value systems, and that democratic values alone might be insufficient. Former authoritarian states seeking to transform themselves into genuine democracies may espouse democratic values but still yield to demagogic temptations that lead them into conflict with other countries. Achieving constitutional liberalism, or democratic means of governance, a more complex task, may be even more important.[1]

A similar sense of identity or self-image, transparency—including military-to-military cooperation—and reasonably healthy economies also may be prerequisites for a stable peace. Experience with cooperation within the European Union—a community of shared values—also suggests that democracies can consolidate a stable peace through a partial pooling of sovereignties.[2]

A nation's sense of its national purpose also must be an influential consideration. A nation bent on political aggrandizement—possible even in a democracy—will not encourage the development of a security community. It will have lost the power to attract and may succeed in excluding itself from a community where equal rights are valued. A major power can become a magnet in attracting other nations to join it within a security community if its value system, methods of governance, culture, and economy are appealing and seem to work. But all that could be lost if such a nation perversely sought to achieve domination over others.

Building a stable peace requires, at some point, a set of understandings, tacit or otherwise, about rules of international behavior. We noted in the introduction the danger posed by practices that generate different sets of norms and expected behavior patterns. A stable peace now exists in the community roughly defined geographically as the western part of Europe and North America: its members have excluded war against one another not just as a rational act of policy, but because such a war has become subrationally unthinkable.[3] Extending a stable peace throughout Central and Eastern Europe has been the stated aim of the North Atlantic Treaty Organization (NATO): three new members have been admitted for the purpose of expanding "the area in Europe in which wars simply do not happen."[4] Although NATO can be a vehicle for supporting the expansion of a security community or for helping to create some of the other conditions for a stable peace—for example, transparency in defense budgets and perhaps a similar sense of identity—it is an insufficient basis for achieving this.

In chapter 5, we argue that a Europe-based joint military structure will be needed for a long time and that we see no reason why NATO could not become the organizational framework to meet this need. We do not assume, however, that Moscow's skepticism about the advantages of NATO enlargement for European stability is just a matter of public posturing. President George W. Bush has said that "Russia is a part of Europe and, therefore, does not need a buffer zone of insecure states separating it from Europe."[5] Given the ambiguity, at least from a Russian perspective, about the purposes behind NATO enlargement, there are clearly limits to the benefits Russia thinks it might gain from having NATO members on its borders. And if Russia perceives itself as a perpetual outsider from NATO councils, a sense of shared identity will be hard to come by. President Vladimir Putin spoke to this point in a joint press conference with President Bush in Slovenia on June 16, 2001: "[O]ur attitude toward NATO was not one toward an enemy organization . . . but . . . we ask ourselves a question . . . [T]his is a military organization . . . they don't want us there . . . it's moving towards our border. . . . Why?"

Until the spring of 1999, wars between nation-states in most of Europe apparently had become almost inconceivable in the minds of some statesmen, who spoke as though war had been overtaken by economic integration, globalization, and the disappearance of ideological confrontation, and who maintained that old-style "great power, territorial politics" was out of date.[6] This vision of the future implied that a stable peace could be achieved through a radical dilution of the role of nation-states in international relations. In this analysis, economic and technological factors had eroded the nation-state's authority from both the top and the bottom. Empowerment of regions or private citizens and enterprises and the sweep of globalization made possible by communications technologies had so altered the framework for human transactions that nations no longer were preoccupied with the accretion of power. War would no longer serve any useful purpose in such a world. One of the unintended consequences of the NATO-Yugoslav war was to call this vision into question, but it cannot be dismissed as illogical; it is a plausible long-term outcome of the globalization process.

The new global agenda—trade and finance, the environment, ethnic conflicts, the terrorist threat, humanitarian and human rights issues, and the spread of democracy—requires close attention by governments, but not at the expense of attention to relations between nations. Achieving a stable peace still depends on interactions between national governments, even though the effects of globalization and technology already have changed the roles of government in some respects. Finding the right balance between policies that concern the direct interaction of the big powers and policies that deal with the newer global agenda is one of the profound conceptual challenges that the major nations now face.[7] Kosovo dramatically illustrated the dilemmas inherent in balancing power politics and the management of ethnic conflict, in balancing sovereignty and fundamental human rights. The Kyoto Protocol on global warming highlighted the tension between national economic progress and international interest in dealing with a common environmental problem. The response to terrorism has shown a keen awareness of the broader security interests all the nations share.

A NEED FOR TRANSITION DIPLOMACY

Remaining from the Cold War are certain vestigial, but still very strong, adversarial attitudes. At this point the extended European system of nations is not undivided. The present divisions could be overcome or reduced to negligible proportions through

1. power preponderance by one nation, most likely a benign, light-handed U.S. hegemony in a situation where Russian weakness and the willing acquiescence of other actors creates, at least temporarily, a peaceful and internally cooperative system; and

2. the flowering of a "democratic peace" throughout the extended European community; that is, a realization of the empirical finding that democracies tend not to go to war with one another.[8]

The first alternative—hegemony—cannot be excluded as a theoretical possibility, but it will not lead to a stable peace. Hegemony would rest, in part, on generalized military deterrence, not on a common value system. No nation in the system—the United States included—could be expected to tolerate indefinitely the relationships implied by military, or even economic, dominance. The second alternative—democratic peace—is more in keeping with Western tradition and, as long as democracy remains deeply entrenched within the major powers, it would be a more lasting outcome in terms of a stable peace. Despite critics of the notion of a democratic peace, the weight of evidence suggests that the notion is valid. However, because fundamental factors like values and self-identity are involved, a long transition period will be required before a stable peace in all of the extended European system can become a reality. During the transition a high form of statecraft will be necessary even to entrench a benign form of conditional peace, a peace free of military confrontation. It should be possible to do this. The recommendations offered in chapter 6 are modest steps in this direction, steps we believe will build momentum behind the idea that a stable peace is a practical goal, beneficial for all nations within the extended European system.

Norms, rules, and structures can be imprinted on an international system even before a stable peace has been achieved. This process will help in the creation of a shared value system. In fact, this type of order-building diplomacy should be the first priority of a statecraft aimed at achieving a stable peace. This is the purpose of the proposals we advance in the final chapter of this book. They are intended to foster the habit of cooperation and to institutionalize it where practicable.

A relatively uniform set of norms and rules throughout the extended European system is a necessary condition for a stable peace. The wars of the Yugoslav succession may be unique in their scale of violence but patches of ethnic or communal strife will be difficult to erase from the map. Small wars can destabilize relations among the major nations within the European system, as Kosovo and Chechnya have shown, and lead to different sets of norms and rules, an outcome that would cause divisions between the nations and work against the achievement of a stable peace. Partly for this reason, such conflicts should be handled within a multilateral framework that includes the European Union, Russia, and the United States wherever possible. It may not always be possible but the exceptions will generate suspicions and the legitimacy of military actions will be found wanting by those left out of the decision making. Multilateral security arrangements, like the network now in the making in the Balkans among the United Nations, NATO, the European Union, and the Organization for

Security and Cooperation in Europe (OSCE), will be essential for collective security purposes even in a system enjoying stable peace.

American, Western European, and Russian policymakers still have an opportunity to construct a post–Cold War order whose internal logic would guide Europe toward stable peace. Regrettably, the West's effort to implement such a policy in the Balkans damaged relations with Moscow just at a time when the need for cooperation had never been more acute. And Moscow's effort to deal with Chechnya shortly afterward set back the relationship still further. Valuable time has been lost. Still, the optimist would say, Russia and the West will have another chance to build a new relationship. The pessimist would say that Moscow and the West are pursuing irrevocably different, and probably conflicting, courses. The response to terrorism since September 11, 2001, has shown that it would be disastrously premature to give up on the effort to secure a stable peace among the major powers of Europe and North America.

Four elements define the equation that governs EU-Russian-U.S. relations: (1) global developments, such as technology and financial and trade transactions; (2) internal developments, in both Russia and the West; (3) specific policies that these nations pursue; (4) specific conflicts or challenges that may arise in other parts of the world, for example, acquisition of nuclear weapons by North Korea or a major war in the Middle East. Machiavelli observed that "fortune is the arbiter of half the things we do, leaving the other half or so to be controlled by ourselves." Among the elements just mentioned, the third—state policies—is perhaps the only one where the governments within an extended European system are dominant. Even an optimal Russia policy pursued with skill and determination by the West, or an equivalent Western policy pursued by Moscow, in short, would not necessarily create the conditions for a stable peace between Russia and the West if underlying trends were not favorable. We believe that, for the present, several underlying trends are favorable and we also think that the contribution of government policy could be decisive in reinforcing the effects of favorable underlying long-term trends.

One important indicator of the possible trajectory of government policies is public opinion. Polling data show that the public, in both Europe and the United States, favors a U.S.-European partnership.

In fact, 80 percent of the Americans polled in 1998 said that the relationship between the United States and the European Union should be one of equal partnership. The public on both sides of the Atlantic has favored including Russia in NATO when Russia has shown that it can be stable and peaceful for a significant period. Public policies can be fully successful only when they are perceived to be legitimate manifestations of national interests. Polls show that policies fostering closer but more balanced transatlantic relations continue to meet this test. And so do Western policies aimed at creating a European security community that includes Russia.[9] Of course, public support for such policies, while broad, may also be shallow, but our point is that there is a receptive climate in the West and that political leaders do not have to overcome public resistance to the politics of inclusion.[10]

THE UNDERLYING TOPOGRAPHY

National policies will have to take into account numerous underlying factors that will influence EU-Russian-U.S. relations. These include

❖ *Demography.* How will generational change affect public attitudes? These changes include (1) the aging of populations, resulting in conflicting spending priorities; for example, more money for pensions and health care, as opposed to support for economic programs, in Southeastern Europe; (2) immigration flows, leading, on the one hand, to greater economic dynamism and, on the other, to pressures to close borders and to organize societies in exclusive ways; (3) the rise of a new generation of Western Europeans for whom the European Union does not have the same appeal that it had for their parents; (4) the rise of a new generation of Russians more attuned than their elders to democracy and a market economy; (5) a future U.S. population in which citizens of Asian and Hispanic ancestry will represent a very sizable proportion, and for whom Europe may not enjoy top priority in foreign policy.

❖ *Geopolitics.* The extended European system of nations could be pulled apart by disparate interests in other parts of the globe. The issue of natural resources, particularly energy and water resources, also can generate conflicts that might affect Europe or North America.

❖ *Technology.* Technology has tended to foster a borderless world, since the revolution in information systems has had an integrating effect at many levels. Different rates of technological progress from country to country, however, may create divisions and raise barriers to cooperation.

❖ *Globalization.* The "invisible hand" of the global economy already has done more to integrate national economies than have government actions, with the important exception of those decisions by governments in Western Europe that have built the European Union, but the disciplines of the global economy are too much for some states currently to meet, while others have resisted them on social or other grounds. The street demonstrations in and around the meetings of the World Trade Organization in Seattle in January 2000 and in Prague in September 2000, and at the EU meeting in Gothenburg, Sweden, in June 2001, show that a strong backlash to globalization has gathered force in recent years.

❖ *Regionalism.* Regions, and states too, cherish their special character, have their own views of how democracy should be practiced, and react defensively against outside encroachments.

❖ *Parochialism and insularity.* A drive for local autonomy and a focus on issues close to home are natural human responses to a global market that is too large and impersonal to identify with in any tangible sense. Thus in some areas borders help to identify and protect ethnic groups.

❖ *Culture.* Culturally determined attitudes must be the slowest to change of all the factors discussed here and could slow the creation of a peaceful, undivided, and democratic Europe. A xenophobic strain of nationalism could push Russia toward confrontation with the West, for example, while in the West some insist that Russia, culturally, is not a part of Europe.[11]

❖ *The influence of the nuclear genie.* Midway through the twentieth century a new technology forced its way into the calculations of nations—the nuclear weapon. It became a major factor in determining whether stable peace could be achieved because it affected the life or death of nations. An important lesson has been learned since the end of the Cold War: it is difficult for nations to be partners within a security community and, simultaneously, rivals in nuclear weaponry. Arms control has little relevance in a case where stable peace exists between two countries since in such a situation there is no reason for an arms race. And arms control is next to impossible in a situation of precarious peace. The case of the Korean peninsula illustrates just how difficult it is. But under a conditional peace, such as has prevailed between the United States and the Soviet Union throughout most of the Cold War and that still exists today between the United States and Russia and China, arms control can be a key element of the relationship, not only in constraining an arms race but also in fostering a broader role for preventive diplomacy. Arms control can be part of transition diplomacy. There are many techniques for achieving restraint in armaments and all of these should be deployed, if necessary, to overcome the nuclear legacy of the Cold War. Otherwise, the nuclear deterrence trap will continue to hold Russia and the West in an outdated adversarial relationship. Both in Russia and in the United States lobbies and vested interests encourage policies that would perpetuate the deterrence trap. Only decisive leadership on the presidential level in both countries will make it possible to overcome the opposition to change. A beginning was made by Presidents Bush and Putin at their meeting in Slovenia on June 16, 2001, when they agreed to launch detailed and serious consultations on the nature of their security relationship.[12]

MODELS OF A FUTURE EUROPE

No one knows how to depict with much certainty, still less how to quantify, a cooperative security order that might emerge within the extended European system of states. Many structures can be imagined, even where conditions generally would seem to encourage stable peace. The shape of a nascent security community centered on Europe is likely to be a lumpy conglomeration of nations—very far from homogeneous. To the extent a shape could be discerned, it would probably be a fuzzy triad—that is, three distinct clusters of states within the system, corresponding to North America, the European Union, and a revived Russia, with other states of the region freely associated, or not associated at all if they so chose, with one or another of these three centers. Power distribution would not be the cause of this arrangement; rather, cultural and geographic factors would. We could imagine a mature security community, something like an enlarged Western community of nations—less lumpy, more homogeneous— but the cultural, historical, and geographic differences within the system will preclude that for a long time.[13]

Furthermore, the major actors—the United States, the nations of the European Union, and Russia—might exert a stronger or weaker influence on events within the system, depending on factors other than whether they themselves are weak or strong. The United States, for example, might remain very powerful and yet choose to exert its influence elsewhere or, if it became isolationist, not at all. The European Union, although it might include some strong nations as members, as noted in chapter 3, might not achieve the unity it needs to exert influence corresponding to its potential. And Russia, even if its current economic illness were cured, might be distracted by internal issues and relations with countries along its southern border.

In the five models described below we sketch in broad strokes several different versions of what may be called a security community. Even though each model posits that all the major nations of the extended European system are democratic and have no military designs against one another, states would act differently under each model. For the sake of simplicity the models are constructed with the United States, Russia, and the European Union as the principal actors, but of course every other potential member of the system would play some part in determining how the model would be constituted. Each model is only a one-dimensional sketch and none are mutually exclusive; in the real world some other combination of the characteristics cited below could appear.

❖ *A triad—the European Union, Russia, and the United States.* The United States retains a powerful economy, fully engaged in globalization, and remains committed to its European ties. Russia, while retaining its own distinctive culture, has embraced democracy, created liberal institutions and a civil society, and adheres to the rule of law; it has built a close approximation of a true market economy, which is generating significant annual growth, and takes an active and constructive interest in European matters. Western European integration is successful, as is the European Union's expansion to the east.

❖ *U.S. dominance.* The United States is first among equals, owing to its greater cohesion and economic strength. The European Union is powerful economically but foreign policy is fragmented. Russia is democratic and is building a society based on democratic means of governance, and its economy is based on market principles but its production of goods and services is not keeping up with its needs in terms of creating a modern society.[14]

❖ *EU dominance.* The European Union is dominant, while the United States and Russia are only loosely engaged with Europe. Russia is democratic but remains weak economically and politically, and is less focused on external affairs than on internal problems and issues involving its southern flank. The United States devotes increasing attention and resources to Asia, Africa, and Latin America; the European Union takes the lead in managing all matters related to Europe, demonstrating consensus and strong, unified leadership.

❖ *A Western commonwealth.* The West integrates while Russia becomes a peripheral player in European affairs. The United States and the European Union develop deeper trade relations and closely coordinate their institutional arrangements. Russia is formally democratic but is experiencing internal difficulties, including the inability of the central authorities to govern effectively throughout the Russian Federation. It seeks strategic partners to the south and east to support its quarrels with the West and with Islamic militants.

❖ *U.S.-European competition.* The United States is dominant but European coalitions, including Russia, are assembled to offset U.S. pressure. Europe is challenging U.S. policies on key foreign policy issues globally and trade competition is fierce. Russia makes common cause with the European Union as necessary to resist U.S. political and economic pressures.

ASSESSING THE MODELS

Even within the European Union, which has established common policies and administrative machinery in a deliberate effort to foster internal unity, national identities remain deeply entrenched. In fact, more variety has emerged within the Union as subregional differences have been allowed to flourish. A security community centered on Europe might create some institutions to facilitate cooperation among the nations, but it is highly unlikely that pooling of sovereignties would occur on anything like the scale that already has been achieved within the European Union. The homogenizing effects of communications, or of globalization, are more plausible candidates for the role of undermining national identities. We have already noted the defensive reactions that can be seen when local or regional groups assert their special character in the face of changes sweeping over them. Nothing short of isolating entire nations from global influences can alter these trends. But despite these influences, historical, cultural, and geographic differences have stubbornly resisted fundamental change. Therefore, fears of losing national identities in a featureless sea of Euroatlanticism seem entirely misplaced. Even if all the unifying elements of a stable peace were in place and functioning well, clear differentiation among groups of states within a security community would exist.

Among these states and groups of states, differing sets of interests will continue to generate different solutions to international problems and, hence, give rise to disputes. Under stable peace, disputes would be settled by resort to negotiation, not by resort to arms. A system based on North America, Russia, and the European Union that had achieved stable peace is self-evidently preferable to the usual state of affairs within this system where peace is at best conditional, often precarious, and wars are frequent. Some models that might seem to promise a stable peace might serve the interests of individual members better than they serve other members. But if a stable peace, under any of the arrangements described above, can be entrenched in Europe in the twenty-first century it would constitute a substantial improvement over the experience of most preceding centuries.

Relations among the members of a security community centered on Europe may be disrupted by events outside the extended European system: the question of peace in Europe is not separable from the question of peace globally. Probably the members of a security community centered on Europe could protect their hard-earned peace more effectively if they were to act on the world stage in some reasonably coherent fashion. An extended European system may one day become solidly democratic from end to end. It could have a broadly shared sense of self-identity and the attributes of a stable peace could be firmly rooted in its culture. With all that said, how would it be constituted? Would it be tightly integrated or would it be simply a loose collection of friendly states that now and then cooperate for some important purpose? A community that was able to act with some degree of coherence in relation to the external realm would be able to achieve things that a disunited cluster of countries could not. At the least it would be less vulnerable to the wedge-driving policies of others.[15]

In short, while the European Union, Russia, and the United States may succeed in making a stable peace among themselves, their relations must also be considered within a larger context. The world's great power centers, or potential power centers, apart from the extended European system are Asian—Japan, China, and India. An equilibrium on a global scale could be encouraged by the construction of a stable peace in the extended European system of nations because Russia and the West would no longer be competing for makeweights. Reconciliation between Russia and the West is an absolute priority from this perspective, and worth a heavy investment.

On the other side of the coin, conflict between a member of a security community centered on Europe and another power outside that system cannot be ruled out. China is a rising global power. Differences on the part of the United States, Russia, and Japan with China already exist to varying degrees. What would be the effect on stable peace in Europe of armed conflict between, say, the United States and China or Russia and China? A neutral policy certainly would be a morally and legally correct policy for other members of the extended European system because the conditions that created a stable peace imply no obligations to come to the aid of a friend in trouble outside the extended European system. The United States fought a long war in Vietnam with little help from fellow democracies in Europe. The existence of a security community centered on Europe ought to be appreciated simply for the fact that Europe would be one less place to worry about. War between any major power within the community and a major Asian power, however, would seriously strain the system, and thus a European security community could be endangered by events in Asia. But if democratic principles and democratic means of governance were firmly embedded in all the major nations of the system, notwithstanding all the special national characteristics that their different histories and cultures would impose, a stable peace within the system probably could be sustained in the face of outside pressures. This is why similar value systems must be the basis for the stable peace we are trying to build.

Our view is that the first model above—a triad—would be the best outcome and the most difficult to achieve. Of all the models, it would most closely resemble a community of equals. The members of such a community would prefer peaceful solutions because similar values and a similar sense of identity pointed them that way. There would be quarrels, to be sure, and winners and losers, as always. But a political structure that enhanced attractive rather than repellent features internally and gave members a sense of equality would reinforce the underlying cultural bias toward peace.

A stable peace already has been achieved in parts of the extended European system, particularly within the European Union. This was not the result of accident or luck but came about because of the vision of Jean Monnet and the coordinated actions of a series of European political leaders down to the present day. A stable peace does not just emerge. It must be shaped by conscious actions on the part of leaders. The task that current and future generations of political leaders in North America, Russia, and Europe must accept is extending that stable peace throughout the whole Euroatlantic community. They will have a good chance of succeeding if they act consistently with underlying trends.

We do not envisage a reduction of norms and values to some nebulous lowest common denominator. To the contrary, we see the necessity of a consensus within the extended European system on democratic values and means of governance. But we also believe that a cookie-cutter concept of national institutions and styles of governance is neither desirable nor feasible; historical and cultural factors have seen to that. And there will be policy differences within a security community, driven by differences in perceptions of national interests. What matters is that disputes and conflicts between nations be regulated by some means other than resort to force. There has been an apparent convergence on that point within the extended European system, certainly among the members of the European Union, and increasingly among the other nations as well. Concerted national policies are needed to reinforce this trend. In the following three chapters we present a Russian, a Western European, and an American perspective on a stable peace that will test whether this much cooperation is possible.

2

The Russian Angle

THE NEED FOR A NEW BEGINNING

A decade after the Cold War was solemnly buried, there is still no stable peace between Russia and the Western countries. Moreover, from the late 1990s the dynamic of the relationship has taken a negative direction. NATO's expansion to the east, the Kosovo crisis, and the second Chechen war stand out as milestones of the gradual slide toward something alternately described as a "cold peace" and a "new cold war." Frustration is steadily building on both sides. Mutual expectations have been drastically lowered. In the Western world, and in North America in particular, public expectations for Russia and its affairs have plummeted. "Russia fatigue" is widespread in Europe as well. In Russia itself, Western, especially U.S., policies are often described as being aimed at keeping Russia weak and fragmented, with a purpose of subjugating it. It would appear, then, that today is anything but a propitious starting point for an effort to chart the road toward a security community centered on Europe that would include Russia.

But such an effort is necessary and should not be delayed. At worst, a Russia that is not properly anchored in a common institutional framework with the West can turn into a loose nuclear cannon.

If conflicts arise between Russia and its smaller neighbors, the West will not be able to sit them out. And a progressive alienation between Russia and the Western world would have a very negative impact on domestic developments in Russia. Now that the German problem has been solved, the Russian problem looms as potentially Europe's largest. The United States will not be able to ignore Russia's strategic nuclear arsenal, and the European Union can hardly envisage a modicum of stability along its eastern periphery unless it finds a formula to co-opt Russia as Europe's reliable associate.

RUSSIAN DEMOCRATIZATION

In the decade since the demise of the Soviet Union and the communist system, Russia has evolved into a genuinely pluralist society, although it is still a very incomplete democracy. To its credit, Russia has a constitution that proclaims separation of powers; it has a working parliament, an executive president, and a nominally independent judiciary. Between 1993 and 2000, three parliamentary and two presidential elections were held; for the first time in Russia's long history, transfer of power at the very top occurred peacefully and in accordance with a democratic constitution. This is already becoming a pattern. Power has been decentralized vertically as well as horizontally. Power monopoly is a thing of the past. Russia's regions have started to form distinct identities. The regional governors, or presidents of republics, within Russia are popularly elected, as are city mayors and regional legislatures. The national economy has been largely privatized. The media, though not genuinely independent either of the authorities or of the various vested interests, are free in principle. There is a large degree of religious freedom, and ideological oppression is nonexistent. Finally, Russians are free to travel abroad.

These achievements are significant, and most of them are irreversible. Yet, Russia's development is handicapped by major hurdles to speedier societal transformation, as is occurring in Poland or Estonia. One hurdle is poor governance, stemming from the irresponsibility of the elites as much as from sheer incompetence. Toward the end of the Yeltsin era, the state itself appeared privatized, with parts of it serving the interests of various groups or strongmen. Corruption and crime are pervasive. Accustomed to living in an authoritarian state, many Russians began to associate democracy with chaos and thuggery. Another major problem is widespread poverty and the collapse of the social infrastructure, including health care. Too many Russians believe they have gained little or nothing from the economic and social changes of the past decade. Taken together, these factors work toward the restoration of some form of authoritarian and paternalistic rule.

The arrival of Vladimir Putin as Russia's second president has been marked by an attempt to reinstate some order by means of strengthening the state, especially the presidency. Putin has also proclaimed the principle of dictatorship of law and approved a set of liberal economic reforms designed to restructure and relaunch the economy. Yet, his recentralization program raises fears of a return to authoritarianism, and his preference for using judicial means to fight his opponents could turn the legal system into an instrument of the executive. Thus Putin's desire to eliminate what he termed the undue influence of a media tycoon on government decision making has resulted in a threat not just to one media empire but to the freedom of speech in general. And, of course, the military operation in Chechnya has so far produced a deadlock that continues to claim lives daily.

In sum, Russia's second presidency is still a work in progress. Putin has been tactically agile and reasonably successful in steadily establishing his authority, but the major decisions—and tests—of his presidency still lie ahead. In the economy, these decisions concern structural reforms, including land reform, and the support for medium-sized and small businesses; in the judicial sphere, revamping the legal system and promoting the rule of law; and in the realm of politics, building a stable party system at the federal level, devising power-sharing formulas between the Russian Federation and the regions, and between the regions and the municipal authorities. Putin's background and his instincts would point to the ideal of a guided, or managed, democracy with the state playing a domineering role. While this may correspond to Russia's historical experience, such an approach will not necessarily make Russia a successful country in the twenty-first century.

However, not everything in today's Russia depends on the preferences of its top leader. The ruling elites at all levels will continue to change relatively fast. The once all-powerful oligarchs have lost much of their influence. Many of the current political figures on all sides already seem relics of the Yeltsin era. The security service officials who have risen under Putin will serve their stint but are unlikely to become a latter-day equivalent of the Communist Party or to stay around for a long time. Regional leaders, despite often exercising an almost feudal control of the provinces, are not immune to electoral challenges.

In a more distant future, the country's fate lies with its nascent middle classes, which are too small and too weak at the moment but which are expected to rise and claim influence if Russia starts to develop its potential in earnest. The population at large, despite the oft-expressed nostalgia for the relative stability and the nominal equality of the Soviet period, largely subscribes to the core values of personal freedom, democracy, and even the market economy. This suggests that the process of Russia's transformation will be very long—measured in generations and decades rather than years—and occasionally bumpy, but that it will generally lead toward consolidation of the elements of democracy and the market.

RUSSIAN PUBLIC OPINION

Public opinion plays a moderate role in Russian politics. On the one hand, Russia is an electoral democracy; on the other, there are few mechanisms for influencing decision-making processes from below. Political participation remains low. Moreover, the ruling elites have mastered the art of manipulating the public. While most Russians take North America and Western Europe as an embodiment of the highest achievements of modern civilization and support good relations with the West, they believe that Russia should not copy Western models and should not become a yes-man to the United States in world affairs. In the wake of NATO enlargement and the financial crisis—to which the unwise policies of the International Monetary Fund contributed —and especially since the 1999 NATO air war against Yugoslavia, anti-Americanism has spread beyond its traditional stronghold among the elites. Great-power mentality, which suffered a major defeat in the late 1980s and the early 1990s, is making a modest comeback. Many young people, for example, angrily accuse the United States of being responsible for what they perceive as Russia's humiliation. Right-wing nationalism has established itself as a permanent political force waiting for an opportunity to move from the margins to the center stage.

Yet, the rise of a Russian fascism bent on revenge is an extremely remote possibility. Nationalism is weakened by a strong imperialist and universalist tradition. Most Russians, moreover, increasingly are preoccupied with their own personal circumstances and focused on personal survival, or success, as the case may be. The process of transformation, for all the pain it is causing, is making Russia ever more compatible with the rest of Europe in terms of values, among other ways. Ironically, to many in the West today's Russia looks ugly because it seeks to be placed in the category of a democratic, law-based, promarket society, and of course it falls far below the current Western standards. But it has made a quantum leap if compared with the late USSR.

RUSSIA'S PLACE IN THE WORLD

Russia believes that its ambition to modernize its economy and to develop a modern society hinges on gaining permanent and easy access to Western investments and technology. Failure to achieve this will probably confine Russia to the far periphery of the twenty-first-century world.[1] The Russian elites aspire to a place among the "civilized nations of the world," which means the West, and its population craves Western standards of living. None of these goals can be attained without permanently and securely burying the hatchet of Russian-Western confrontation and establishing an environment of stable, not just conditional, peace.

Our working assumption is that stable peace between Russia and the West is feasible. Their core interests are broadly compatible, even if interaction is still difficult. Their cultures are close enough for mutual understanding and interaction, although trust must be nurtured for some time. In any event, large-scale wars or permanent politicomilitary confrontations between Russia and the West can be safely declared to be a thing of the past. It does not follow, however, that stable peace is at hand. At best, it is no less than three or four decades away: the time required for effecting fundamental changes in Russian society and polity, for a new generation to come to the fore, and for the establishment of properly functioning joint institutions. Positive changes will not arrive automatically, and so we are talking about thirty to forty years of sustained effort. Thus the actual time frame could well be longer—or slightly shorter if we are very successful. Ultimately, however, everything will depend on the nature and direction of Russia's domestic transformation.

Even if the direction of socioeconomic and political change is generally positive or broadly encouraging, simply presiding over the "process" is not enough. To accomplish something way beyond the time horizon of even the youngest among the currently active politicians in the West and Russia, vision is required of the caliber possessed by the men who built stable peace within Western Europe and created the transatlantic community. One means of enlightening the future protagonists of the Russian-Western partnership is education and dialogue. Such dialogue, moreover, needs to be part of the structure of the rapprochement. The important first step is to define a clear set of objectives on the way to establishing such a dialogue.

In this chapter, we explore the nature of the problem of the Russian-Western security relationship; examine the security interests of both partners and identify areas of convergence that can serve as stepping stones to a more benign, if still conditional, peace between them; and, finally, outline in broad terms the strategy and tactics that would create or rearrange the building blocks of a future stable peace.

THE NATURE OF THE PROBLEM

The problem in the Russian-Western security relationship can be summarized as follows: Having ceased to be adversaries, the two failed to become partners and face the prospect of estrangement. Early attempts at partnership have failed because neither side was yet ready to engage on the terms acceptable to its would-be partner and, more importantly, found it hard realistically to formulate its own terms. The enmity of the previous era manifests itself in lingering suspicions. The results are sad. Russia and the West warily face each other as neither foes nor friends. "Strategic partnership," oversold and underdeveloped, has become a meaningless phrase. Uncertainties about the future course of relations are pervasive.

Both sides bear their own heavy responsibilities for this false start, but complaints are usually directed at the would-be partner. Most members of the Russian elites fault the West for self-serving triumphalism following the end of the Cold War. They point out that the forty-year confrontation was brought to a close by joint efforts, with the Soviet Union voluntarily paying the ultimate price of dismantling itself. While the West capitalized on the peace dividend, Moscow had to bear the brunt of massive demilitarization. It turned the key on German reunification; dissolved the Warsaw Pact; withdrew its forces from Central and Eastern Europe; allowed the former satellite countries to pursue their own foreign and security policies; let free the Baltic republics, even without insisting that all their Russian residents be made eligible for future citizenship; and saw the Soviet armed forces divided up. All this, the Russian elites would insist, went unappreciated.

The situation is compounded by the fact that a security community is being expanded rapidly, but without Russian participation. The countries of Central and Eastern Europe and the Baltic states are in the process of joining European and Euroatlantic institutions, such as the European Union and NATO. The end of the Cold War has led to the security integration of the Soviet Union's former satellites and several of its republics within the enlarged West, but this integration has so far excluded the principal successor state of the USSR. That the Russians continue to be kept out of the European Union and NATO has led most of them to view NATO expansion as unfriendly and EU enlargement as more of a challenge than an opportunity.

Moreover, where NATO is concerned, this effort is aimed at least in part at deterring residual or hypothetical future threats from Russia. While the reasons behind the decision to open the Alliance to the east have less to do with these would-be threats, the reasons for seeking accession to NATO are firmly rooted in the historical experience of the countries lying between Russia and Germany. The strong feelings and expectations involved are most frankly discussed in the Baltic states, including by their highest officials. It is interesting to note that in neighboring Poland the perception of insecurity has markedly decreased following that country's admission to NATO in 1997. Now the Poles are ready to begin building bridges to the east again in search of a new equitable relationship—from the position of a *Western* country.

The future enlargement of the European Union, which Moscow initially welcomed as an alternative to NATO's expansion, raises the prospect of Europe's economic, political, and security integration reaching all the way to the Russian border. Russia faces the very likely prospect of becoming the only country in Europe that is not part of the Union or associated with it (as Ukraine would like to be). As a result, the barrier between Russia and the rest of Europe may rise higher.

While Russian membership in either NATO or the European Union is not formally foreclosed (both President Clinton and NATO secretary general Lord Robertson referred to the possibility), its prospect is usually downplayed as irrelevant for the foreseeable future. In private, it is often simply dismissed. Even if one believes that Russia will at some point be invited into the Alliance or the Union, one has to accept that this can happen only after all Russian neighbors are admitted and successfully integrated. The prospect of a Ukraine in NATO, when Russia is not (or even "not yet"), is inherently destabilizing. Thus, security building in Central and Eastern Europe has a serious downside, which is the de facto exclusion of Russia.

One needs to make a clear distinction between NATO membership, where political factors come to the fore, and membership in the European Union, where practical, chiefly economic, obstacles have to be cleared. Nevertheless, the feeling of being excluded is a very powerful one. Even if it does not lead to aggressiveness, it may well lead to self-isolation. A failure of Russia's Euroatlantic project logically leads it to embrace Eurasianism—not as a philosophical concept, but as a pragmatic response to its security needs. The evolution of the Shanghai Five over four years from regularized summitry into an institutionalized security forum with a tendency to expand its membership is very indicative of the trend.[2] Building the structures of stable peace is closely linked with the fundamental question of strategic identity. This question in the post–Cold War world is, Does Russia intend to stand alone, align itself with the West, or attempt to cobble together an anti-American alliance with China and other states in Asia and the Middle East?

For the past three centuries, Russian rulers have viewed their country as a European/Eurasian/global great power, wielding enormous military strength. It entered into coalitions with other powers in Europe and beyond, but these coalitions were usually short-lived and did not encroach upon Russia's strategic independence. With the end of the USSR, the situation has drastically changed and Russia for the first time in centuries is weaker militarily than the major powers and alliances in Europe and Asia. Russia cannot hope to change the balance of power and therefore has to come up with a novel answer to its security problem. Yet, much of the current Russian strategic thinking reveals very traditional patterns.

Russia's strategic thought has two principal empirical sources: the Soviet Cold War experience and the practice of the Russian empire. The Soviet military superpower, ever ready to prevent America's military superiority, sought to enhance Russia's security by means of direct physical control over the zones of key strategic importance to Russia, such as Eastern Europe and Mongolia. The Soviet strategic culture required complete obedience from its nominal allies, which were reduced to the status of satellites. From this perspective, the loss of even the former allies to NATO leads to two very pessimistic conclusions: (1) NATO will advance eastward to box Russia in and subject it to increasing pressure; and (2) Russia not only has lost its superpower status, but is being denied its rightful position as a major power in Europe. Its interests are not taken into account because of its current weakness.

Russia, of course, is no Soviet Union, and the Russians are fully aware of this. An attempt to construct a new Moscow-led alliance within the Commonwealth of Independent States (CIS) yielded very limited results, and the plan to enter into a dialogue with NATO from a psychologically more comfortable position of the leader of a group of countries never got off the ground. Still, many members of the Russian security establishment carry an outsized view of their country's strategic role. That Russia might be merely a regional power is anathema to them. To them, it is a great power, a "pole" in the multipolar world, and, potentially at least, a global player.

The Russian conception of the multipolar world, which has been emphasized less since the arrival of President Putin, was actually based on the notion of a balance of power among several centers of influence. The very fact that this concept was used as a strategy to undermine and block the presumed U.S. ambition to establish its world hegemony suggests that some in the Russian leadership continue to view the Western threat, represented by the United States and NATO, as the principal strategic challenge, even if it is overshadowed for the time being by the threat of Islamic extremism.

In many ways, the late Romanov period is the closest parallel to the intellectual environment prevailing in the Russian security community at the turn of the twenty-first century. Realpolitik is back, as is self-reliance. Alexander III's famous dictum, "Russia has only two true friends in the world, the Russian Army and the Russian Navy," is now inscribed on the walls of the General Staff Academy in Moscow. This emphasis on strategic independence in an essentially friendless world is also a reaction to the perceived naïveté of Gorbachevian promotion of mankind's interests (to the detriment of Russia's, it is implied), and the alleged knavely subservience of Foreign Minister Andrei Kozyrev's diplomacy. Geopolitics in its classical late-nineteenth-century form has succeeded Marxism-Leninism as the guiding body of thought for most Russians involved in security policymaking.

This Russian strategic *Alleingang* has deep historical roots but is tinged with a sense of mission. The Russians pride themselves in having saved Europe from conquest several times in the past eight hundred years: first from the Mongols, then from Napoleon, and more recently from Hitler. In this spirit, they claim that in Chechnya and Central Asia they have become a barrier defending Europe from Islamic extremism and international terrorism. To some, Europe's apparent thanklessness only enhances Russia's moral superiority.

Behind this bravado, however, is a country deeply pessimistic and unsure of itself. Its outward assertiveness masks a very unfocused strategic posture. The famous 1999 dash by two hundred Russian paratroopers to seize the Pristina airport in Kosovo, ahead of the NATO forces, was an indication of Russia's weakness, not its strength. The threat issued in 2000 to bomb the Taliban camps in Afghanistan revealed the lack of a clear and credible strategy in Central Asia. The set of policy papers released in 2000 and purporting to set strategic guidelines for years ahead (the national security concept, the military doctrine, the foreign policy concept, and a few others) reads more like a series of textbooks for young diplomats, civil servants, and officer cadets than operational documents. Statements of priorities are conspicuously lacking, and the reader remains confused.

THE WESTERN VIEW OF RUSSIA

Typically, Russia's ambivalence vis-à-vis the West is mirrored by Western attitudes toward Russia. Above all, Americans and Europeans categorically reject any Russian claim for "compensation" for the dismantlement of the "evil empire" as sheer nonsense. Eventually, the Western governments conceded a special status to Russia in its relations with NATO (the Permanent Joint Council) and the G7 (G8). They emphasized, however, that a voice was not a veto. Meanwhile, the image of the country in the West has changed from highly positive in the aftermath of the official discarding of communism to bleak and negative at the start of the Putin presidency.[3] It is not so easy to define Russia's place in the security strategy of the West.

The second war in Chechnya, begun in 1999, has cast a long shadow over the perception of Russia in the West. Moscow's response to the Chechen provocation was universally condemned in America and Europe as disproportionate, brutal, and insensitive to the fate of the hundreds of thousands of civilians-turned-refugees. Russia's territorial integrity was not in question, but the methods of preserving it were deemed to be grossly uncivilized. Russia, admitted to the Council of Europe in 1996, faced censure with the prospect (however remote) of suspension, faintly reminiscent of the Soviet Union's expulsion from the League of Nations in 1939. It is ironic that Russia was most severely criticized by the European Union, the Council of Europe, and the OSCE—the three organizations Moscow had clearly preferred as prime shapers of Europe's post–Cold War order. The protracted guerrilla war in the North Caucasus, with no victory for either side in sight, is likely to remain not only Russia's bleeding wound but also a persisting irritant in Russian-Western relations. Russia's appeals to the West to close its eyes to the brutalities of the war in the name of a common front against international terrorism will be rejected. Moscow's self-image as a bulwark of civilization against the forces of extremism will not hold up if the war cannot be ended.

SOURCES OF WESTERN ATTITUDES

In the United States, insularity is growing. Ironically, in view of the Russian fears, Pax Americana is *not* the way most Americans see the world. Globalization and provincialization go hand in hand. Even old allies are receiving less attention than they did during the Cold War. There is no new grand design, with a place set in it for Russia. Gradual withdrawal into itself is the prevailing trend in the United States, unilateralism is becoming the preferred if-we-must-act option, and building new alliances, especially with the former principal adversary, is beyond the pale.[4] Engaging Russia was tried and not liked. Excessive optimism about Russia and intrusiveness in dealing with it (however benign) were shown to be most unhelpful.

Russia, of course, was not "lost" by the United States. Unlike Germany and Japan, Russia had never been defeated militarily, occupied, or ruled by the Allies. Its elites had never been reeducated, and its public had never been given the benefits of a new Marshall Plan. The relationship had never been steeled in a forty-year conflict with a common foe. As an exceedingly difficult customer, with the potential to destroy the political reputation of any U.S. administration that dared to move too close to it, Russia slipped down Washington's list of priorities. It became all but irrelevant to some of the principal issues of U.S. security policy: NATO enlargement, crises in the Balkans, and deployment of a national missile defense. A nuisance, Russia could not be engaged. A weakling, it could be safely ignored.

Europe's main preoccupation in the 1990s was with its domestic affairs. The unfolding of Project Europe demanded increasing self-concentration. The Maastricht and Amsterdam Treaties, the Schengen agreement, and the introduction of the euro marked a new stage in the Union's development. A common foreign, security, and defense policy started to emerge, but the Russia factor barely figured in the Union's calculations. The Union's "Common Strategy" toward Russia was at least as much a product of the Union's internal transformation (and in particular its adoption of a Common Foreign and Defense Policy and European Security and Defense Identity) and of the prospect of its future expansion to the east, as of any Russia-specific interest. As the first post–Cold War decade drew to a close, Russia was neither a threat nor an opportunity to its closest Western neighbors. Apart from the German business community and the Finns, with their thirteen-hundred-kilometer-long eastern border and an unparalleled expertise in handling Moscow, there are apparently few in Europe who are paying serious long-term attention to Russia.

Russia fails to capture the imagination of the Europeans—for the first time in one hundred years. It is no longer the hotbed of a world revolution. It is no longer the darling of the leftist idealists and the bogeyman of the conservatives. It is no longer the valiant ally, but neither is it a would-be invader, presumed capable of marching to the English Channel in less than seven days. The "evil empire" is no more, but no "Russian miracle" is in the pipeline. Instead, at the edge of the continent Europe faces an unhappy peripheral country that has sorely failed in its first misconceived, misguided, and mismanaged attempt at reform. In short, Russia is an uninteresting mess.

COMMON SECURITY INTERESTS AS STEPPING STONES

A mess, indeed, but not one that can be safely ignored. Common security interests do exist between the West and Russia and must be

identified and consolidated to form a basis for a future common security regime—or security community—leading to a stable peace. To
begin with, one must recognize the differences in the strategic environ-
ments of Russia, Europe, and America that result in substantially different security agendas.

While war in defense of one's territory has become unthinkable
for much of Europe (hence the crisis of Western European militaries)
and is being conceived—and practiced—only in defense of interests
and values (as over Kosovo), things are very different on its eastern
periphery. Russia is less secure by far than its would-be partners,
and its principal security problems are of domestic origin. There is also
no stable peace anywhere on its borders. Peace is conditional in the
west, precarious in the south, and uncertain in the east. In Chechnya,
there is war. Even Russia's nominal allies in the Collective Security
Treaty are posing risks to its security, owing to their domestic instability or ethnic conflicts.[5] For Russia, a global war is as remote as it is
for the West; wars, however, are back and have become a grim reality,
even a routine. For the past twenty years, Russia has been almost constantly at war with different groups of *mujaheddin* in Afghanistan,
Tajikistan, and the North Caucasus.

An analogy of sorts can be drawn with France of the 1950s, which
had to fight in Algeria and Indochina. Russia, however, is not separated
from its battlefields by great distances. And the Chechen war is a long-
term engagement, while Dagestan and Ingushetia are not out of the
danger zone. Russia's involvement in the conflicts in Central Asia and
Afghanistan has become a reality. As the Russian leadership demon-
strated in 1999–2000, it is willing to fight back or even threaten preventive military strikes: war can serve a useful political purpose, helping
mobilize popular support for a candidate of the ruling clan. Many Russians feel that this grim strategic environment is not appreciated by
the West, especially by the Europeans, who demand that the Russians
follow postmodern norms of warfare. The Russians reply that, with the
enemy that they face, the kind of forces that they have themselves,
and the environment in which they are fighting, warfare can only be
of the traditional kind. However, the clear and present danger in the
south carries a blessing in disguise.

Of Russia's three strategic fronts, the western one is the least threatening. Few Russians fear direct NATO aggression against their country. There are even fewer people who would regard the European Union as a future source of military threat. The modified Conventional Forces in Europe (CFE) Treaty virtually rules out a surprise large-scale conventional attack against Russia from the West. It is true that NATO's air war against Yugoslavia over Kosovo and the Alliance's 1999 strategic concept have raised the prospect in many Russian minds of Western military involvement in conflicts along Russia's periphery, or even on its territory. Any hypothetical Western military intervention in Russia, however, is thought to be reliably deterred by its huge nuclear arsenal. What does not impress the assorted rebels securely bars entry by the world's mightiest powers. America's plans to build a national missile defense system are unlikely to jeopardize the Russian deterrence capability in the foreseeable future. Thus even the skeptical but sensible Russians would agree that they are safe from the West.

Acting upon this conclusion, a pragmatic Russian government might decide, if just for the purpose of economy of forces, to promote reconciliation in the west and concentrate on the vulnerable southern flank. (Reconciliation in the east has been successfully practiced since 1989.)[6] There is some historical evidence supporting this option.

During the nineteenth century, Russia engaged in prolonged peacetime security cooperation with the major European powers. One example was the Holy Alliance in the first half of the century, which sought to bolster the monarchical principle anywhere on the continent in the face of revolutions; the other was the *Dreikaiserbund* in the century's second half, which opened the prospect of an amicable relationship among Europe's three big empires: Russia, Germany, and Austria-Hungary. Having thus secured peace in Europe, Russia in both cases became very active in the Caucasus and later in Central Asia. Yet stable peace was still not possible. Alliances broke up and wars ensued. Of course, these historical examples have left some bitter memories (as in Hungary after 1848–49), and anyway it would be absurd to call for a new kind of a directoire, however disguised, for Europe. The point is that, historically, Russia and its Western neighbors could be allies in peacetime as well as war.

Today, Russia and the West share key security interests that allow for close and sustained cooperation. Their overriding interest is the prevention of major war and confrontation in Europe. Russia has as little appetite for confrontation as the Western countries. Moreover, there are no resources available to support a large-scale defensive effort. For the first time in half a century, Russia stands outnumbered in Europe by the Western alliance. Its defense industry is barely producing hardware, and most of what it produces is for foreign customers. The demographic situation also remains highly unfavorable for Russia.[7] The qualitative gap between Russian and NATO forces (in terms of levels of technology and of education of personnel) is as wide as at any time since the Crimean War. Unable to fight a conventional war, Russia will be compelled to "go nuclear" early in any serious conflict in the west. This is a very powerful incentive for Europe and America to proceed to demilitarize the relationship.

Russian-Western differences over ethnic conflicts in the Balkans and the Caucasus are well known. It is essential to note that much of what each side sees in the "other side's" actions as part of some grand design with far-reaching and usually ominous implications is the result of a failure at conflict prevention, misconceived attempts at crisis management, and the weight of extraneous (mainly domestic political) factors. The use of force by NATO against Yugoslavia was preceded by a singular failure of Western and Russian leaders to agree on a common approach to the Kosovo conflict. The cracks in the Contact Group, which included the major Western powers and Russia and had served as a vehicle of Balkans policy coordination among them, were immediately exploited by Yugoslav president Slobodan Milosevic. The message is clear. Joint conflict prevention, management, and resolution are in both sides' interests, which will be ill served by continuing instability or by their taking different sides in conflicts that are less than critical to their core interests. Transatlantic and Eurasian security could and should be linked by joint peace operations. So far, the only examples of this have been in the Balkans (with the IFOR and SFOR operations in Bosnia and the KFOR operation in Kosovo). In the future, this cooperation could be expanded to include Russian-European operations in such places as Moldova and the Caucasus.

Proliferation of weapons of mass destruction and missile technology occupy different places on U.S., European, and Russian security agendas. For the United States, these are about the only threats that can jeopardize its security. For Europe, the spectrum of danger is wider and the assessment of the nuclear-biological-chemical missile threat more conservative. For Russia, the threat posed by proliferation is very high, owing to the country's geopolitical situation, but it is considered to be far less serious than other dangers the country faces. In spite of the disturbing implications for strategic stability that the U.S. plan for a national missile defense represents for the Russian-American and Russian-Western relationships, there exist opportunities to limit the damage at the strategic level and cooperate on the level of theater missile defenses (TMD).[8] European, Russian, and U.S. interests in the eastern Atlantic and Mediterranean can be threatened in the future by missile-armed regimes or groups.

The opportunity to cooperate on TMD points to yet another potential interest, namely, defense industrial cooperation between Russia and the West. Moscow has proposed using the Russian S-300 air defense system as a basis for developing a new TMD system. Future systems could be deployed on ships and based on the boost-phase intercept principle, and thus be both flexible and nonprovocative. If this were to happen, Russian-Western security cooperation would acquire for the first time a meaningful economic and technological basis. The Russian defense industrial complex, now even more anti-American due to the ruthless competition on the world's arms markets, would moderate its position, with clearly positive political implications.

Finally, there are common threats presented by international terrorism and religious extremism. The situation in Central Asia and Afghanistan will require continuing coordination of Russian, U.S., and EU efforts to combat threats to regional stability coming from the likes of Osama bin Laden. Russia is already engaged on this score with the states in the region and China. It would be shortsighted to view the Russian-Western relationship in this region as though it were a revival of the "Great Game" of the nineteenth century, when the great powers vied for preeminence in the region.

Adding it all up, these common interests are compelling to various degrees. The strongest one deals with the elimination of major wars and prevention of confrontation in Europe. Regarding regional conflicts, the situation has been much ameliorated with the departure from power of Milosevic, who was a major irritant in Russian-Western relations. It has become possible to cooperate in consolidating democracy in Serbia and helping Serbia manage its relations with Montenegro. Russia and the West also have cooperated in facilitating Yugoslavia's return to the world community. On proliferation there is agreement in principle, but sharp disagreement between the United States and Russia (and to a far lesser extent between the United States and Europe) over the ways of dealing with the missile threat. Crisis, rather than cooperation, looms on the horizon. Defense industrial cooperation is difficult to achieve and remains very limited even among NATO Allies. It takes a real optimist to hope that trilateral cooperation can be achieved on the TMD issue.

Regarding terrorism, of course, one man's terrorist is often another man's freedom fighter. Islamic extremists allegedly have links with people in Chechnya. But Moscow's attempts to assign the Chechen rebels to the camp of international terrorists or their agents and for a long time to reject the idea of negotiations has weakened the credibility of its calls to form a common antiterrorist front. The situation has seriously soured Russian-Western relations.

It is also important to note again that the extended European system is not the only one to which Russia can and does belong, and that Russia must watch its other flanks. Moscow seeks to create a web of bilateral and multilateral security relations with the CIS countries and perceives NATO and U.S. activism in the former USSR as unwelcome competition. Russia is also trying to create a stable and cooperative environment in its relations with China. This factor should not be downplayed. A conflict with China, now considerably more powerful than its northern neighbor, would spell disaster for Russia, and Moscow would do anything to avoid it. But there are also indirect threats. The future evolution of U.S.-Chinese relations, in particular with respect to the Taiwan issue, will have important repercussions for Russian-U.S. relations.

Lastly, there are vested interests living off Russian-Western tensions. The Russian military establishment draws its prestige (and its budget) not from the Chechen-type contingencies, but from the potential U.S. or NATO threat. Conversely, the residual Russian threat forms the rationale for much of the U.S. defense potential capacity, and for U.S. forward presence in Europe. Along with China, Russia is considered to be the principal nuclear threat to the continental United States. European countries on Russia's western periphery continue to view their neighbor to the east as the only credible military threat. The countries of Eastern and Central Europe retain vivid memories of Soviet domination. None of this is likely to change very soon.

GLOBALIZATION

Russia is definitely not among the leaders of the process of globalization. Yet, consider the following: Russia's foreign trade amounts to 40 percent of its GDP; some sixty million people cross the country's borders in both directions annually; and the collapse of the Russian stock market and the ruble in 1998 were directly precipitated by the Asian financial crisis. Whereas the Soviet Union almost through its end was effectively isolated from the outside world, the Russian Federation from the very beginning has been a part of it. This is a fundamental change with far-reaching implications.

Many of the consequences of this new openness have been negative. Russia has lost tens of thousands of its world-class scientists and specialists, who left to work and live in the United States, Western Europe, and Israel. At the same time, Russia has borne the burden of accommodating hundreds of thousands of refugees who emigrated from the zones of conflict in the Caucasus and Central Asia. Whole industries have collapsed, unable to withstand foreign competition. The U.S. dollar, replacing the indigenous ruble, has become the de facto currency of Russia.

Yet, Russia still possesses certain advantages it could use to find its niche in the globalizing world. Although its exports are predominantly raw materials, its most valuable resource is its reasonably well educated workforce. The continuing high levels of science teaching and the fast rise in economic and financial education are encouraging. Having failed to become a postindustrial country, Russia may have a chance of advancing in the era of knowledge-based economy. Other advantages derive from Russia's geographic position as neighbor of the expanding European Union and the dynamic countries of East Asia. Its borders, once barriers protecting the USSR from the "hostile capitalist environment," could become interfaces for cooperation and integration. Finally, the sheer enormity of the task of rebuilding Russia will require massive foreign investments, which are likely to flow from the outside world once the domestic conditions in Russia are right.

ROADS TO STABLE PEACE

The fast track to a stable peace between Russia and the West failed. The West was not prepared for the long march of Russia's transformation and expected results too soon. The Russian elites refused to accept what they had come to regard as Pax Americana, that is, a unipolar world. There is little likelihood that they will accept this model a decade later. As noted above, the long-term option of letting a stable peace grow naturally as a by-product of Russia's democratization is unsatisfactory. First, time may be not on the side of stable peace supporters. Democratization is a risky process. Fledgling democracies are unstable, and occasionally can be warlike.[9] Second, this approach is too deterministic. To borrow a Gorbachev-era phrase, Russia and the West are not doomed to live in stable peace. A mid-term strategy is called for.

Even though all roads to a stable peace are arduous, the journey must be taken. Practical things first. For Russia, the principal element of peacebuilding should be the expansion and deepening of relations with the European Union, using the Union's enlargement as a stimulus. A partnership with the Union worthy of the name will minimize whatever problems Russia will have with NATO. Russian membership in the Union is not an issue, but, as a matter of principle, it should not be excluded. For Russia, becoming part of Europe is essentially a domestic project. It means establishing the rule of law, securing human rights, building a functioning democracy complete with institutions of civil society, and becoming economically compatible with the rest of Europe. All these goals can be achieved internally, and to the extent that they are, Russian-EU relations will gain a solid foundation. Relations with Brussels can be strengthened by means of joint security projects, but the modalities will largely depend upon the degree of security policy coordination within the Union. It would only be right to keep this cooperation open to the Americans and even *encourage* them to come aboard. In this context, Russian-EU rapprochement may become key to European autonomy in defense and security matters. In principle, a permanent association between Russia and the European Union, built around a free-trade zone and a system of privileged political consultations, is feasible. Eventually, this would come to be a true security community. Stable peace would at last be at hand.

Relations with NATO look less promising for Russia, but they should not be ignored. Russia may not be invited to join NATO any time soon. Still, Russia and NATO are cooperating to fight terrorism. Russia is involved in two NATO-led operations in the Balkans. Should there be a joint TMD project for Europe, NATO would likely be involved. The Russians should formulate positive policy objectives with respect to NATO. Until recently, the objectives were mostly negative—from the desire that the Alliance dissolve itself to barring NATO enlargement to the east. If the Russians can come up with a list of goals they can attain in cooperation with NATO, the whole atmosphere of NATO-Russian relations will change. Russia and NATO should avoid squabbling over cooperative decision making and concentrate instead on actions that deal with twenty-first-century threats and facilitate Russian military reform, which is long overdue.

In the final analysis, only a prosperous and self-confident Russia can move toward a security community centered on Europe. By the same token, only a Russia that has a functioning civil society, practices the rule of law, and shares fundamental values with the West can instill confidence in its would-be partners. Mutual trust can be built only in a step-by-step manner and through close constructive engagement, but this incremental method of building a stable peace has a good chance of eventual success.

The ability of the Western countries to influence the pace and direction of Russia's evolution is notoriously very limited. It is especially challenging to influence Russian developments in a *positive* way. Of the instruments available to the Western governments and publics, helping Russia to become "wired" to the global information network is one of the more powerful. Drastic expansion of Internet connections from high school upward is bound to yield dramatic results over time. Creating tens of thousands of stipends for Russian students, enabling them to receive education in Western Europe and North America, will ultimately provide Russia with a modern-thinking elite, even if many of those students choose not to return home after graduation.

CONCLUDING REMARKS

Building stable peace between Russia and the West is primarily a civilian task. It is up to their respective societies, their institutions, and their individual members to form qualitatively new links. The defense and national security establishments can play only marginal roles, and their impact, especially at the beginning, can be negative. However, to give the civilian forces a chance one must work to dismantle the vestiges of military confrontation between Russia and the West. This is a crucial condition. Demilitarizing the relationship would undermine the ability of undemocratic, obscurantist, and corrupt forces in Russia to capitalize on Cold War memories and the loss of Russia's great-power status while empowering those who seek to promote the rule of law, make the economy transparent, and check crime and corruption. It would also bring to an end the present situation, in which Russia treats the European Union as a partner and the

Atlantic Alliance as a potential adversary. It would allow reform of the Russian military so that it could address the likely challenges of tomorrow, rather than remain ensconced in a threat environment that no longer exists.

Europe can be peaceful, undivided, and democratic if those taking up the cause equip themselves with patience and perseverance.

3

Western European Attitudes

I N OUR INTRODUCTION TO THIS BOOK we referred, for the sake of simplic- ity, to the European Union as a principal actor in the various models of a security community we described. In chapter 1 we chose a "triad" consisting of Russia, the European Union, and the United States as the best outcome for a European security community. It should be realized, however, that the European Union, despite its name, neither covers all of Europe nor constitutes a union in the internationally accepted legal sense. Some European countries have chosen not to belong; others cannot—or cannot yet—join. Moreover, the Union does not have a government but is governed by a European Council, con- sisting of the heads of state or government of its member-states. Its only supranational body, the European Commission, has indepen- dent competence only in matters regarding the common market in the widest sense and cannot speak for the Union on political matters.

This diversity makes it that much more difficult for the leader- ship in Europe to work toward a stable peace. While working on inten- sifying relations within the Union, and on the accession of new mem- bers, the Union must at the same time try to reach common views on the relations of its member-states with the United States and Russia. The danger is that, overwhelmed by their immediate problems, which are challenging enough, European statesmen will lose sight of the more distant goals of a stable peace.

It is time to consider what can be expected of the Union, what it has achieved, and where it is heading. We have to consider whether the Union can speak for Europe and whether it can do so with one voice. The relationship between the Union and NATO will influence the viability of the security area that we have in mind and thus needs to be studied, especially in light of the intention of the European Union to set up its own common defense policy and to establish its own rapid deployment force. Finally, we must pay attention to the Union's relationships with the United States on the one side and Russia on the other.

There are three intergovernmental organizations besides the European Union that can play a role in endeavors to reach a stable peace: the North Atlantic Treaty Organization (NATO), the Organization for Security and Cooperation in Europe (OSCE), and the Council of Europe. A fifth one is about to disappear: the Western European Union (WEU). We deal with each of these in turn.

EUROPEAN UNION

When the visionary Frenchman Jean Monnet made plans for the future of Europe shortly after World War II, his main purpose was to ensure that war on the continent, especially between France and Germany, would become impossible. His goal, in other words, was a stable peace, although this expression had not yet been formulated in the sense in which it is used in this book. In his view, a European federation should be the final outcome, but he realized that this idea could hardly be accepted so shortly after the war. He therefore devised a "step-by-step" approach. The participants would take a single step toward a united Europe each time sufficient public support could be found. In this way, first a Coal and Steel Community was formed by six European nations in 1952. Then slowly a common market was created and expanded by the admission of new states, until the present European Union with fifteen members was attained. War between the member-states has indeed become unthinkable and a stable peace does exist inside the Union. The Union, however, is far from exercising an influence on the world scene commensurate with its size. During the last years of the twentieth century and the first of the twenty-first, the European Union took steps toward a common foreign and defense policy in order to increase its influence.

Common European Foreign Policy

In 1970 the European Economic Community (as the Union was then called) adopted a report on European political cooperation (EPC), which proposed to strengthen member-states' solidarity on major political problems through meetings between their diplomatic services. This indeed led to closer cooperation in international bodies and multilateral negotiations. After an EPC secretariat was established in 1986, the number and scope of joint foreign policy declarations increased. However, every word of every declaration still had to be approved by the foreign office of each member-state.

By adopting the Maastricht Treaty—which came into force on November 1, 1993, and was revised by the Amsterdam Treaty, which entered into force on May 1, 1999—the members of what was then named the European Union agreed to work toward establishing a common foreign and security policy (CFSP). This project has been described in an explanatory document of the high representative (entitled "The Council of the European Union and the Common Foreign and Security Policy") as "the integration project of the next decade."[1] In June 1999 former NATO secretary general Javier Solana was appointed high representative for the CFSP. In March 2000 a new Political and Security Committee at ambassadorial level started work on a permanent basis in Brussels to give impetus to the common foreign policy and elaborate a common security policy. Solana was the logical choice as chairperson, but it was decided that the representative of the country holding the presidency should exercise that function. The fact that not Solana but the European Commission member for foreign relations, Chris Patten, disposes of the huge sums that the Union spends on development aid and aid to the countries of Central and Eastern Europe weakens the influence of the high representative even more.

The Amsterdam Treaty further provides that the European Council (the highest organ of the European Union, consisting of heads of state and government) shall decide on CFSP strategies in areas where the member-states have important common interests. On the basis of these strategies the Council of the European Union (consisting of the foreign affairs ministers and the high representative) can adopt decisions, actions, or common positions by a qualified majority. But if a member opposes one of these decisions "for reasons of important national policy," the question goes back to the European Council and is decided there by a unanimous vote.

In other words, the Maastricht and Amsterdam Treaties have taken a step forward compared with the EPC. In the Nice Treaty of December 2000, the Political and Security Committee in Brussels was given formal status and charged with drafting common strategies in foreign affairs. It remains apart from—but is associated with—the European Commission. The adoption of such common strategies, however, still depends on the political will of the member-states to work together. On the basis of an adopted strategy a common foreign policy can then, in theory, be implemented by majority vote. Whether this will actually happen remains to be seen, since the exception cited above makes it clear that member-states remain free to establish their own foreign policy and to deviate from the common policy if they so wish.

The aforementioned explanatory document of the high representative recognizes that "the political will that is evident when treaties are being negotiated is not always followed by day-to-day political will when the Union has to act on the international stage." To bring together sometimes very divergent national interests into one common and mutually binding policy would imply that member-states give up an important part of their sovereign power to decide their own foreign policy. There is as yet no indication that the larger member-states of the Union, in particular, are prepared to do so. "The Council of the European Union and the Common Foreign and Security Policy" admits that member-states' foreign policies "have not, of course, disappeared." It even asserts that it is not the purpose of the CFSP to make them disappear. Clearly, this will make the achievement of a Euroatlantic security community that much more difficult. For some time to come the United States and Russia will have to deal with different actors on the European scene trying to project European power through policies on which they have not yet agreed.

A common strategy for bilateral relations between the Union and Russia was adopted at a meeting in Cologne held on June 3–4, 1999 (discussed at pp. 62–64). Draft strategies for other countries or regions were held up by fierce controversies between member governments. Strategies regarding the Middle East and Ukraine were finally approved in 2001. It is a time-consuming process. The EPC practice of issuing laboriously hammered-out common statements that enshrine the lowest common denominator of divergent views on the issue in question will probably continue. The only step forward will be that those views will be mutually influenced and perhaps aligned to a greater extent than before, now that there is a permanent commission for this purpose. This commission's existence will exercise a certain pressure on national governments to come to agreement; parliaments and public opinion can sometimes be persuaded to accept unpalatable foreign policy decisions in the name of European solidarity. But for the time being, diverging views of individual countries will have to be taken into account and no European official, nor any statesman of a member country, can speak for the whole. Solana is able to make foreign policy pronouncements only if the policy has been approved by all members beforehand. Moreover, although he did succeed in establishing himself as political spokesman and even negotiator for the Union, he has to compete with both the chairman-in-office of the Political and Security Committee and the European Commission member for foreign relations. Still, he has been able to carve out a prominent position, especially in the Balkans.

If Europe wants to speak with one voice in foreign policy affairs, there is no better subject with which to begin than Euroatlantic relations (as discussed at the end of this chapter).

Common European Security and Defense Policy

A common security policy has to be based on, and could hardly exist without, a common *foreign* policy. Occasional decisions to exercise force can be—and have been—taken jointly by all (or some) of the members of the Union. But such decisions do not amount to a common security policy. Moreover, some members of the Union have declared that they are unwilling to participate in such a policy because they consider themselves to be neutral. "The Council of the European Union and the Common Foreign and Security Policy" therefore states that a common security policy would "not affect the specific nature of the security and defense policies of certain Member States" and would be "compatible with the policy conducted under the North Atlantic Treaty"—the only time NATO is mentioned in the document. This looks very much like trying to square the circle.

Common Defense Forces

A European entity, whether called "union," "federation," or "confederation," will eventually have—and is entitled to have—its own defense force. This in itself need upset neither the NATO Allies that are not members of this entity nor Russia. U.S. policymakers from President Kennedy onward have stressed the need for the European allies to carry their defensive weight in the Alliance. The question, therefore, is not whether a strengthening of European defense forces is desirable but whether there is sufficient political will to allocate the necessary resources and whether a European force can be established in such a way that it does not impinge on, or duplicate, the unified command structure and the political and military coordination within the Alliance.

An EU summit conference held in Helsinki on December 10–11, 1999, "underlined its determination to develop capacity to take decisions and, where NATO as a whole is not engaged, to launch and conduct EU-led military operations in response to international crises." The Helsinki communiqué added that "this process will avoid unnecessary duplication and does not imply the creation of a European army." By 2003, a sixty-thousand-strong force will be made available by member-states on sixty days' notice. Non-EU European NATO members and "other interested states" (this would include Russia) may contribute to what is called "EU military crisis management."

A military committee and a force headquarters have already been established in Brussels. But most of the sixty thousand troops will remain under national command until a joint decision for action has been taken. Countries participating in the military force structure of NATO have emphasized that their rapid reaction forces will remain assigned to NATO as well. Any improvement of those forces would therefore also benefit NATO. Complete "transparency" between the EU force and NATO has been pledged.

Nevertheless, inconsistencies remain in the claims of European politicians regarding a common defense policy and common defense forces. For instance:

❖ Many politicians try to convince their own publics that a common defense policy exists and that a common defense force, capable of rapid, independent military reactions in crisis situations, will soon be operational. In reality, a common defense policy on which such actions could be based does not exist. Moreover, it is generally recognized that those European forces that would eventually be combined into a common rapid reaction force lack sufficient equipment for electronic intelligence, mutual communications, and rapid (air) transportation and are still deficient in such areas as nighttime fighting, precision-guided bombing, and the use of spy satellites.

❖ Although improvements are foreseen, these forces cannot as yet operate independently of NATO (indeed, chiefly U.S.) assistance in these areas, as was shown in the Kosovo conflict. The possibility of some member-states taking joint action without full NATO participation but with NATO support in these areas was established at the NATO summit in Berlin in 1996. The Washington NATO summit in April 1999 decided that such action could be conducted under EU command. But, obviously, other NATO members—and the United States in particular—will have to approve the use of NATO means, even when they themselves do not want to commit forces to the intended action. It may well take ten to twenty years before the European Union has enough rapidly deployable and sufficiently equipped air, naval, and army forces to use them independently and in an integrated way without NATO (i.e., U.S.) help.

❖ The same politicians maintain, with an eye on public opinion in several EU member countries, that this force will not constitute a European army, although this is obviously the final intention of several member-states, in particular France.

❖ They claim that the Kosovo experience has shown the need for closer European defense cooperation. The truth is that it has shown that European rapid reaction forces available to NATO need to be quickly upgraded to the technical standards of U.S. forces—which can be done only with U.S. technological support. It is possible that the new ideal of EU military cooperation will relax some budgetary restraints. In some European parliaments the conviction is growing that the end of the "peace bonus" has been reached and that defense expenditure cannot be further diminished. Still, it remains very doubtful whether sufficient political support can be found for the huge additional expenditures that will be necessary if European militaries are to match the technological capabilities of U.S. forces.

❖ Politicians claim, with an eye on the U.S. Congress, that the EU force will not duplicate any of NATO's functions. Despite such denials, financial and manpower resources are being spent that might otherwise have been devoted to bolstering NATO.

Unrealistic expectations are thus being created and, at the same time, anxieties are being aroused in the United States and among other NATO Allies that are not members of the European Union.

A pledging conference held in Brussels in November 2000 did little to fulfill the expectations or allay the anxieties. Participants offered to put some one hundred thousand troops at the European Union's disposal, but it has been estimated that up to two hundred thousand need to be made available to keep sixty thousand men and women in the field for a year. Remarkable was the pledging of forces by six countries, including Turkey, that belonged to NATO but not to the European Union. Nine prospective members of the Union also made offers. President Vladimir Putin had already promised Russian "cooperation." The equipment on offer turned out to be as varied in type and quality as might have been expected, underlining the fact that

Europe's forces are still far from possessing the cohesion, strength, or armaments needed to sustain a prolonged military engagement. No political agreement exists about the role the European forces will play. While the German, British, and Dutch ministers, among others, reaffirmed the primacy of the U.S. connection via NATO, the French stressed the "political control" and the "strategic guidance" they hope the Union will exercise. The current and future U.S. administrations will have to decide—probably on a case-by-case basis—under what circumstances and on what conditions European-led operations will be allowed to borrow NATO equipment and intelligence. The operations in Macedonia are a case in point.

The establishment of an EU rapid deployment force that eventually could act on its own thus could divide the Alliance if not handled with great care by both the European Union and NATO. The big remaining question is whether planning for independent EU military actions will take place within NATO or outside it. Planning within the allied military headquarters is difficult for France, which is represented at NATO headquarters but has chosen not to participate in NATO military cooperation. Planning outside the Alliance, however, would lead to duplication in *optima forma*.

EU Enlargement

Expansion of the European Union toward the east will undoubtedly contribute to a more stable Europe. New members have to accept and abide by the rules and regulations of the Union. The feeling of belonging to the large community will restrain nationalist and extremist elements in new member-states, which will in turn influence the way in which those states deal with neighboring countries and treat their minorities. It is for this reason that the United States is strongly urging the European Union to accept new members as soon as possible. Washington should realize, however, that accession to the Union is a very difficult process for both the new members and the Union and that it necessarily will take time. The Union needs a thorough administrative overhaul before it can admit new members, as will be discussed later. It also needs a new agricultural policy, since, as is generally acknowledged, application of the existing policy to new members will create an unworkable situation. The prospective new members, for their part, will have to show that they have a working political democracy that respects human rights and the rule of law. They will need to create in their economies a functioning free market, able to withstand competition from the existing members. Last but not least they will have to accept *acquis communautaire,* the rules and regulations now in force in the rest of the Union. For the United States to try to force the pace may prove counterproductive.

In the autumn of 2000, the European Commission drew up a "road map" for the admission of new members. It was based on the hope that the internal reform of the Union's institutions could be decided upon at the EU summit conference in Nice in December 2000 and would be ratified by the existing member-states not later than 2002. It was thought that accession negotiations with some or all of the members of the first group of candidates could also be completed during 2002, assuming they would by then have met the criteria for admission. This group consists of Cyprus, Estonia, Hungary, and Slovenia, with the Czech Republic and Poland lagging somewhat behind. There was even hope that some members of the second group (consisting of Bulgaria, Latvia, Lithuania, Malta, Rumania, and Slovakia) would be ready for accession negotiations during 2002. Successful candidates could then be admitted individually, and their admissions ratified by the existing members, in time for the elections for the European Parliament in 2004, or at least before January 1, 2005; when the mandate of the present European Commission ends.

The EU summit in Gothenburg on June 15, 2001, confirmed this schedule,[2] although many observers continued to regard it as too optimistic, particularly in light of a referendum conducted in Ireland just before the summit, which rejected the Nice Treaty. This result made another referral to Irish voters necessary and could prompt second thoughts elsewhere in Europe, thus delaying ratification procedures in other countries as well. Long transitional periods will anyway be needed before those admitted become fully integrated into the Union.

Turkey has been designated a candidate but does not yet fulfill the preconditions for membership, so negotiations with that country have not yet started.

Expansion of the Union was generally welcomed by public opinion in the present member-states when it was first proposed. Few people realized the tremendous costs that the addition of states with much lower standards of living would entail for the European Union. When these costs become known, they may well make the eventual ratification of accession treaties difficult. Furthermore, trade unions have already expressed anxiety over the influx of cheap labor from the new member-states, notwithstanding the growing recognition in Western Europe that additional workers are needed. Europeans as a whole are getting older and retiring earlier, while the number of young people entering the workforce will be insufficient to keep it intact. Germany and Austria have demanded that the right of free entry for workers who are citizens of the new member-states be restricted for the first seven years after admission of those states into the Union. Other countries oppose this on principle, however, since a basic right of the Union is involved. It is therefore uncertain whether such restrictions will in the end be applied. There is also anxiety about the transfer of labor-intensive manufacturing to Central Europe. In fact this is already happening on an increasing scale. But this is probably an economically desirable development that should encourage the governments of the older member-states to stimulate retraining of their workers for careers in sectors with a higher added value per worker, such as services and information and communications technologies.

Worries about a greater influx of illegal immigrants and criminal elements are better founded than those about an influx of legitimate workers. The eastern borders of new member-states will have to be much more closely guarded before the free flow of persons established by the Schengen agreement can be applied in Central Europe.

The European Union and Russia

By far the most important European state outside the European Union is, of course, the Russian Federation. Can it and should it eventually join the Union? No democratic European state is excluded from the

Union. But some Russian leaders have indicated that they would not want to surrender their big-power status in order to join. Anyway, Russia would have to better apply the principles of the rule of law and show more respect for human rights than it does presently. Moreover, it would have to go through an enormous economic restructuring before it could ever hope to comply with the rules and regulations of the Union. Russia is not barred from membership but the practical obstacles to its admission seem to be insurmountable for the next several decades.

The present relationship between the European Union and the Russian Federation is guided by two documents:

❖ the Agreement on Partnership and Cooperation (PCA) between the European Communities, Their Member-States and the Russian Federation, which entered into force on December 1, 1997; and

❖ the "Common Strategy of the European Union on Russia," dated June 4, 1999.[3]

The latter of these consists of three parts:

❖ the European Union's vision for its partnership with Russia;

❖ areas of action; and

❖ specific initiatives.

The "Common Strategy" paper makes clear that the members of the Union are prepared to cooperate with Russia to ensure a stable, democratic, and prosperous Russia in a united Europe free of new dividing lines. It offers help in consolidating Russian democracy and the rule of law and in integrating Russia into a common economic and social space in Europe. It proposes cooperation to strengthen stability and security in Europe and beyond. It also proposes common development of energy policies and sustainable natural resources, joint efforts to combat crime and illegal immigration, and much more. In short, Europe extends an open hand to Russia, a hand offering considerable support. Many proposals, however, seem too intrusive and may well run against Russian nationalistic feelings.

The section "Co-operation to Strengthen Stability and Security in Europe and Beyond" specifies that "the EU wishes to deepen and widen co-operation with Russia and identify common responses to the security challenges in Europe and beyond" through

❖ reinforcing political dialogue by "considering ways to make the existing political dialogue more operational and develop joint foreign policy initiatives" (apparently the existing dialogue has so far not been very substantive);

❖ "cooperating in the elaboration of a European Security Architecture, within the framework of the OSCE, and of a European Security Charter";

❖ "considering facilitating the participation of Russia when the European Union avails itself of the WEU for missions within the range of the 'Petersberg tasks'"[4] (Kosovo revisited);

❖ "enhancing EU-Russian cooperation to contribute to conflict prevention, crisis management and conflict resolution, promoting arms control and disarmament and the implementation of existing agreements, reinforcing export controls, curbing the proliferation of 'weapons of mass destruction' and supporting nuclear disarmament and destruction of chemical weapons."

Cooperation between the European Union and Russia on security issues can help overcome Russian hesitations and prevent unnecessary misunderstandings by identifying common responses to the security challenges in Europe. However, when discussing these problems, and especially challenges beyond Europe, care should be taken to avoid any impression that participants are "ganging up" on the United States.

Part III of the "Common Strategy" elaborates specific initiatives and is the shortest of the three parts, because member-states could not agree on any more detailed version of this section. Its content is not only meager but also repetitive in that it again discusses improving the existing political dialogue. Help to bolster Russia's economic recovery, to improve its investment climate, and to expand two-way trade is promised.

The European Union and the United States share the desire to help Russia achieve prosperity, democracy, and stability. They should endeavor to work more closely together and to coordinate their efforts to reach these goals. However, both have had a tendency to intrude more than is necessary into the internal affairs of the Russian Federation. Assistance should be made available but not imposed.

Russian reactions to EU enlargement have not been unfavorable. President Putin has actually stated that he welcomes EU plans to admit new members from formerly communist Central and Eastern Europe.[5] Moscow apparently does not consider the prospect of admission to the European Union of states that used to belong to the Soviet sphere of influence, or even to the Soviet Union itself, as disadvantageous to present Russian interests.[6] A very large percentage of Russian exports to the European Union are made up of oil and gas, products that the European Union will need after enlargement as much as before. Russian manufactured goods now exported to members of the former Soviet bloc may face higher tariffs and more competition if and when those states join the European Union, but Russia may also find a larger unified market for its products. According to Putin, the European Union now accounts for 35 percent of Russian trade. This would rise to 50 percent when the European Union absorbs members from the former Soviet bloc.

The Russians have also reacted favorably to the establishment of a European rapid reaction force and Putin has even promised to cooperate with the force. It appears that the Russians have concluded, correctly, that this force is in no way directed against them.

Economic Relations between the European Union and the United States

Some Americans, members of Congress in particular, seem to have been surprised when U.S. trade negotiators were suddenly faced by European counterparts speaking and acting in the name of fifteen European nations. Accustomed as they were to dealing with individual European allies that they had helped to put back on their feet after World War II, they failed to realize that a European community had arisen with

joint foreign trade policies. The commissioner in charge of trade negotiations has behind him the clout of the largest trading bloc in the world.

In fact, the United States and the European Union are each other's
most important trading partners—but also each other's greatest com-
petitors. Since the Union has its origins in common economic and agricultural policies, while pleas for protectionism are common in the
United States, it is hardly surprising that trade conflicts have arisen
between them. At first, those conflicts were rooted in the desire on the
part of both sides to protect markets. Now, however, health protection
and even ethical questions play an important role on the European
side, while some U.S. measures taken in the field of foreign economic
policy have clear foreign policy overtones. These extraneous considerations have made it more difficult to reach agreements.

Both sides have been at fault. The European attempts to protect
banana growers in former colonies in the Caribbean, for instance,
were clearly against the rules of the World Trade Organization (WTO).
Those growers should, if necessary, be given direct support, not the
protection of special import tariffs. The United States, for its part,
should have realized that genuine fear of the health effects of geneti-
cally altered food (whether warranted or not) was at the basis of
European import bans on such food, not protectionism. U.S. "carousel
sanctions"—prohibitively high import duties on different goods from
different countries every six months—would seem to be a very blunt
axe with which to punish the Europeans. The Union has also complained to the WTO that these duties are not in accordance with
WTO rules. The Iran-Libya Sanctions Act and the Helms-Burton Act, as
enacted by the U.S. Congress, showed a lack of understanding for the
rights of citizens and the sovereignty of other countries. Sanctions
have to be imposed multilaterally, not unilaterally, and this means
that preliminary consultations are required.

In view of the enormous size of both markets, economic measures
taken by one side can easily inflict serious economic and financial
damage on the other. The magnitude and the close interdependence
of the transatlantic market, therefore, constitute both strong and
weak points in the U.S.-EU relationship.

Some progress has been made. The United States and the Union agreed upon a "New Transatlantic Agenda" in 1995. It provided for intensified cooperation in four main areas:

- ❖ furthering worldwide peace, stability, democracy, and development;
- ❖ jointly combating terrorism, environmental pollution, and other common dangers;
- ❖ contributing to expanding world trade and closer economic cooperation; and
- ❖ improving transatlantic understanding—for example, by nongovernmental dialogues and scientific cooperation.

A Transatlantic Economic Partnership (TEP) was launched in 1998. In this framework an early warning mechanism was established in June 1999 to detect potential economic conflicts and to stimulate efforts to resolve them. Scores of expert meetings are regularly held in the framework of TEP, at both governmental and nongovernmental levels, where multilateral and bilateral subjects that affect their relations are discussed. All these activities culminate in high-level meetings twice a year, one on each side of the ocean, which have proved to be valuable instruments for solving old problems and launching new ideas.

The conflicts that have occurred have not fundamentally undermined transatlantic relations. Both sides are convinced that close cooperation, not just on security but on foreign trade as well, remains essential. Nevertheless, foreign trade conflicts will continue to demand constant attention to prevent them from becoming more serious than is warranted.

The Future Development of the European Union

A European Union that may eventually consist of thirty or more states clearly cannot be governed by a European Council in which thirty prime ministers have an equal say and an equal veto. More decisions will have to be taken by majority vote—but which decisions, and how many votes would each member get? A European Commission that would continue to include two nationals from each of the larger states and one from each of the smaller states would no longer be workable —but which member-state would acquiesce in not having a commissioner of its own nationality? To solve these problems, an Intergovernmental Conference (IGC) of representatives of the present member-states set to work on institutional reform of the European Union.

But when the results of the IGC were debated at a summit conference in Nice in December 2000, it soon became clear that no joint decisions on fundamental institutional reform of the European Union could be made. Since each proposal that would have allowed the European Council to make decisions on one of the more important subjects by a majority of votes was vetoed by one of the larger member-states, agreement was reached only on a small increase in the categories of subjects that can be so decided. After long wrangling, agreement was reached on a new but very complicated voting system that gives the four larger member-states slightly more influence and introduces a "blocking minority" based on population sizes that gives additional power to Germany. This system will hardly improve the transparency of the decisions of the European Council for the general public. The rules for membership of the European Commission will be left unchanged upon the admission of new members until a maximum of twenty-seven members is reached, although it is clear that there are already insufficient tasks for so many commissioners and that the efficiency of the Commission will suffer as a result. The European Parliament was again enlarged by the decisions made at Nice both to accommodate representatives from the new member-states and to allow an increase in the representation of the unified German state. (This in spite of the fact that the Parliament was generally considered to have already too many members.) But it was not given more power.

The proposal to accept new member-states was not controversial and was adopted as expected. The approval in principle of the formation of groups of members willing to go further in their cooperation or integration than the others ("core groups") may well turn out to have been the most important (or fateful) decision made in Nice.

Thus the European leaders have failed to show any long-term vision. Every leader has seemed more interested in protecting his own country's sovereignty than in building a European Union. The old Gaullist idea of a "directorate" of larger nations seems likely to rear its head again. Representatives of those nations gathering before every council meeting, secretly or openly, will "precook" the decisions to be made in the full council. In the eyes of the smaller members, and of the new ones especially, this would be the worst outcome. The people of Europe will in the end not accept being governed by small groups they do not see as "theirs," and that are neither transparent nor democratically controlled. Realizing that their work remained incomplete, the European leaders decided that a new Intergovernmental Conference would be convened to prepare further proposals to be presented in 2004.

It seems more and more difficult to continue taking small steps. The time for more radical changes has come. But which direction should such changes take?

There have always been two views of Europe's future: that of a federal Europe, as envisaged by the founder of the European movement, Jean Monnet, and that of a Europe of states, as proposed by the late French president Charles de Gaulle.[7] It is to the great credit of the German foreign minister, Joschka Fischer, that he reopened the debate on this question in a speech (called "personal") in Berlin on May 12, 2000.[8] He was the first European statesman in a long time who dared to use the word "federal" again and to draw the conclusion that in the end only in a federation based on a constitutional treaty could the rights of all European citizens be guaranteed. Only in this way, he said, could further erosion of support for the Union by the average European citizen be prevented. This federation would have full sovereignty, but the nation-states would not disappear. The federation would be based on—and cooperate with—the member nations. Thus sovereignty would be divided between Europe and the nation-states. The principle of "subsidiarity" (always legislating at the lowest appropriate level) would be enshrined in the constitution. This would ensure that only those questions that demanded a European solution would be dealt with at the federal level and that all the rest would be left to the individual states. Thus the existing states would, in Fischer's view, maintain a considerably stronger role than the Länder in the German Federal Republic.

Fischer imagines three phases. First, those countries prepared to work together more closely would increase and strengthen their cooperation. Second, this "core group" might conclude a basic European treaty that would be the starting point for a later federal constitution. This basic treaty would foresee a strong council of ministers that could speak for the group as a whole. It could be formed either out of the European Council (and thus consist of representatives of national governments) or out of the European Commission but with a chairperson chosen directly by the citizens of Europe. The European Parliament would become bicameral. One chamber would be elected directly, as it is now, and one would be chosen by, or consist of members of, the national parliaments. Fischer also foresaw the function of a president for Europe, to be chosen by its citizens. The core group would be open at all times to other states wanting to participate. The creation of the European federation would be the third phase. The difference with the step-by-step approach is that there would be agreement beforehand about a final goal.

Are the European peoples ready to embrace this vision? Most are obviously not. Reactions to Fischer's speech showed the almost instinctive distaste for the word "federation" in the United Kingdom and opposition to the idea in many other member-states. The German foreign minister will therefore not have been surprised that his initiative was immediately opposed by the prime ministers of Great Britain and Spain and that he was accused of "dreaming."[9] Many politicians, looking at the immediate future rather than the long term, expressed fear that Fischer's vision would disturb the already extremely difficult negotiations within the IGC. Such considerations were prominent in first reactions from, among others, the Dutch state secretary for foreign affairs and the French prime minister.

Almost a year after the "personal" speech by his foreign minister, German chancellor Gerhard Schroeder gave his views, not as chancellor but as chairman of his Social Democratic Party.[10] He followed the ideas of his foreign minister to a considerable extent. Like Fischer, Schroeder proposes a council of ministers, which he thinks should be formed out of the European Commission. The European Council should become a second chamber of the European Parliament, a senate or federal council. His proposals elicited generally unfavorable reactions. Support came only from the Belgian, Finnish, and, to a lesser extent, Italian governments (and the Italian government was voted out of office shortly afterward).

French president Jacques Chirac gave a lengthy and considered answer to Fischer in a speech to the German parliament in Berlin on June 27, 2000.[11] Not surprising for a follower of de Gaulle, he strongly emphasized the role of the nations in the Union. Not a "United States of Europe" was his goal, he later explained, but a "Europe of united states." The word "federal" did not appear in his speech. Still, he endorsed the idea of a constitution for Europe and the formation of "core groups," for which he coined the new term "pioneer groups," of nations willing to work toward "strengthened cooperation." As for potential areas for more cooperation, he suggested the economy, defense and security, and the fight against crime. Foreign policy was missing. In his view, a new treaty, as proposed by Fischer, was not needed. His thoughts therefore, although not unconstructive, did not go nearly as far as those of Fischer. In fact, many of his ideas had already been suggested by other French politicians. Still, a minister in the government of Prime Minister Lionel Jospin thought it necessary to emphasize that what his president had said was not French policy.[12] The dualism in French "cohabitation" politics once more reared its head.

The French prime minister himself waited more than a year after Fischer's speech to explain his own thoughts on Europe's future, on May 28, 2001.[13] He listed a great number of ideas, some new, many well known ("protect European culture") or obvious ("combat crime"), and others that sounded as though they had been taken straight out of a socialist election speech ("protect trade union rights"). He emphasized his ideas about "economic coherence" and "social solidarity" that, according to him, demanded a European "social treaty" and "strong and efficient public services." A long-term European defense strategy should be defined, thought Jospin, "in particular to adopt a coherent position to meet the controversial initiative of the United States to create an anti-missile shield." His political choice was "to make Europe without unmaking France." Not to be outdone by Chirac, he invented yet another expression for European unification: "federation of nation-states, combining the federal idea with the reality of the European nation-states." In fact there was no discernible difference with the "Europe of united states" foreseen by Chirac. Jospin acknowledged that his idea was ambiguous from a legal point of view but, he said, "Europe is an original political construction, combining two different elements: the federal ideal and the reality of the European nation-states." The French prime minister tried, in other words, to bend slightly toward his German counterparts but in fact opposed most of what they had proposed.

The British prime minister, Tony Blair, presented his vision in a speech in Warsaw on October 6, 2000.[14] He recognized that before, as he put it, "plunging into the thicket of institutional change," we should first ask the basic question of what direction Europe should take. He saw no profit "in pitting the European institutions against intergovernmental co-operation." Europe needed a strong commission, he emphasized, and the European Parliament was a vital part of the checks and balances of the European Union. Blair then stressed that the Union had to be more than just a free trade area, like NAFTA in North America. He added: "Europe today is no longer just about peace. It is about projecting collective power." But he also stressed that "the difficulty with the view of Europe as a superstate . . . is that it too fails the test of the people." The British prime minister here applied an old trick: ascribing to an opponent an extreme idea that nobody had advocated and then opposing it. Certainly Fischer did not have a "superstate" in mind. However, he did use the word "federal," which is so abhorred in England.

Blair called Europe "a unique combination of the intergovernmental and the supranational." Fischer could not have agreed more. But the question remains as to what the balance between the two should be. Here, Blair pulled back and seemed to contradict his point of departure: "We should not therefore begin with an abstract discussion of institutional change." Making several practical proposals for changes in EU institutions and rules, he rejected the idea of a European constitution but accepted a statement of principles, a "kind of charter of competencies." A second chamber of the European Parliament would consist of representatives of national parliaments who would review the European Union's work. Blair had no problem with groups of member-states going forward together, but he urged that such groups be open to the accession of other member-states.

Blair's views, it seemed, were closer to those of Chirac than to those of Fischer, although he left many questions unanswered. But he did make it clear that he believed the Union needed reshaping and that he wanted to play an important role in this process.

The enormous diversity of opinions expressed by European leaders makes clear that the new IGC that has to work toward agreement on these issues in 2004 has its work cut out for it. However, its point of departure is different from that of the IGC that led to the Nice summit. First of all, the Nice summit showed that Fischer was correct when he said that the step-by-step approach may be nearing the end of its useful life. In the second place, the largest member-state, Germany, has now clearly initiated a debate on whether the final goal of European unification should be a federation or a loose conglomeration of states. Many observers, accustomed to the step-by step approach and weary of grand designs, believe that it is highly premature even to discuss federalism for Europe. Europe is unlike the United States, they emphasize, in that it is composed of nation-states that have grown up independently for centuries, and it has no common language. It is interesting that many other politicians throughout Europe seem not so much opposed to a loose federation in principle as wary of the debate itself, which they fear will interfere with their ongoing work and for which they suspect their fellow citizens are unprepared.

It will take many years before a majority of European citizens are likely to subscribe to Fischer's and Schroeder's ideas (as those two men have themselves recognized). In addition, issues such as the introduction of the euro, the admission of new members, the regulation of the entry into the Union of refugees, reform of the agricultural policies, and institutional reform leave little time for leaders of the Union to contemplate bold moves toward federation.

Yet a point has now been reached where it is increasingly difficult, if not impossible, to continue step by step, without an overall view of where Europe is headed. Fischer and Schroeder may well have pointed toward the only route Europe can take if it wishes to be truly and democratically united.

Could such a democratic unification be furthered by the creation of "core" or "pioneer" groups as sanctioned at the Nice summit? Creating core groups would carry a risk of splitting rather than uniting Europe, especially if it were done, as the French president suggested, outside the existing Union treaty. New member-states might feel that, just having entered the Union, they were once more being left behind. However, those countries desirous of faster cooperation or further integration could not be expected to wait the ten, fifteen, or even twenty years it would take the new members of the Union to catch up.

A majority of the peoples of Europe express a favorable attitude when asked about European integration. Many Europeans of all ages believe strongly that Europeans belong together, provided that their continent remains democratic and they have a say in how it is run. The development of a European Union has seemed to falter many times before, only to be revived, sometimes with surprising jumps ahead, such as the signing of the Schengen agreement on free movement across borders and the introduction of the euro as a common monetary unit. It is to be hoped that the flame of Jean Monnet's vision has not been entirely extinguished. Perhaps new visionary leaders will be able to gather enough public support to carefully work out plans in a core group within the existing Union. This group could sow the first seeds of a federation, to be joined by the other member-states later. Clearly, it would be a long-term process.

NATO

The North Atlantic Treaty Organization (NATO), a mutual security system between Europe and North America, was set up on April 4, 1949, as an alliance for collective defense against the perceived aggressive intentions of the Soviet Union. Since NATO's declaration in 1990 that it would no longer regard the members of the Warsaw Pact as its opponents, its character has changed fundamentally. It has adopted new rules of engagement and undertaken peacekeeping activities "out of area" in the Balkans.[15] Furthermore, three Central European nations that used to belong to the Warsaw Pact have been accepted as members, while many other Central and even Eastern European states have stated their intention of seeking to join the organization.

The incorporation of the three Central European states into NATO prompted more debate, especially in Western Europe but also in the United States, than did the possibility of EU expansion. Not everyone was convinced that such a piecemeal extension of NATO was wise. It was bound to upset the Russian public, while helping to stabilize only part of Central Europe. Once those three states were accepted, debate died down. Still, the addition of these and other Central European states will entail bringing their forces up to NATO levels of proficiency, which will be very costly for the countries involved, as well as for NATO itself. Nevertheless, many commentators believe that it is necessary not to let the other applicants for membership wait too long if the Western stabilization effort is to be continued.

It should not be forgotten, however, that while it has not been overly controversial within NATO itself, NATO expansion has met with much greater Russian opposition than has the proposed expansion of the European Union. This opposition is fed partly by nostalgia for the days of Soviet greatness: the fact that the border with the Atlantic world has moved so much nearer is a vivid illustration of the weakening of Russian power. The fight against NATO expansion is a powerful rallying cry for nationalists. That NATO has no aggressive intentions is not always believed by elderly Russians, who have been exposed to Soviet propaganda for so long. At the same time, there is also a genuine feeling among democratically minded Russians that NATO enlargement tends to exclude the Russian Federation from the European security scene.

Accession to NATO of countries that formed part of the Soviet Union will be a particularly sensitive issue. As we discuss in chapter 5, the Baltic states for the time being pose the most imminent and serious problem in this regard.

To counter Russian objections to NATO expansion, the West has tried to bridge the mental gap still existing between Russia and the Alliance. On May 27, 1997, a Founding Act Concerning the Mutual Relations, Cooperation and Security between NATO and the Russian Federation was signed in Paris. Chapter I of this document describes the principles that form the basis for a partnership between NATO and Russia. Chapter II established a new body: a Permanent Joint

Council encompassing all the NATO Allies and Russia. This council is supposed to meet regularly (in reality it does not) and constitutes the forum for discussion of all outstanding problems between Russia and the West. It remains completely separate, however, from the North Atlantic Council.

NATO actions against Serbia increased the existing antagonism toward the West in Russia, not so much because of a mystic Slavic solidarity as because of a feeling that Russia was bypassed as a major power and a permanent member of the UN Security Council when Western air attacks on Yugoslavia were not sanctioned by a UN resolution. Later the Russians thought—rightly or wrongly—that having materially contributed to the capitulation of Yugoslav president Milosevic, they had been promised or at least were entitled to their own peacekeeping zone in Kosovo. In general, the conflicts in Bosnia and Kosovo have shown that peace-enforcing and peacekeeping operations in Europe should not be carried out while ignoring the Russians. Russian participation can establish precedents for future cooperation, help in the creation of a system of shared values, and provide a forum for the discussion and resolution of conflicts.

The Permanent Joint Council did not function well during the Kosovo crisis. Russia first withdrew from the council altogether, and when the Russian representative returned, he refused for some time to discuss anything but the Kosovo conflict. Russia may have had reason to feel bypassed, but no conflict can be solved when one side walks out. However, even if the Permanent Joint Council could have functioned more constructively, the fact remains that it is not empowered to assist in the type of order-building diplomacy that, as underlined in our introduction, would be required to establish a stable peace.

Could Russian membership in NATO solve these problems? The working assumption of this book is that eventual Russian membership in NATO should not be excluded as a viable road toward stable peace. In 2000 the presidents of Russia and the United States, as well as the secretary general of NATO, discussed the prospect. Early in the year Putin, who was then the acting president of Russia, stated in an interview that he did not exclude the possibility of NATO membership for the Russian Federation. How serious he was remains to be seen;

Putin has shown a tendency to make pronouncements to suit his counterpart of the moment. U.S. president Bill Clinton, for his part, was very clear in the address he delivered when he accepted the International Charlemagne Prize 2000 in Aachen Cathedral on June 2, 2000.[16] Discussing the prospect of "Europe whole and free," he said,

> no doors can be sealed shut to Russia—not NATO's, not the EU's. As Winston Churchill said when he received the Charlemagne prize in the far darker days of 1956, "in a true unity of Europe, Russia must have her part." . . . We must build real institutional links with Russia, as NATO has begun to do. Of course, it won't be easy, and there is still mistrust to be overcome on both sides, but it is possible and absolutely necessary.

NATO secretary general Lord Robertson in May 2000 was more cautious when he gave an interview to a Russian radio station. He stated, "I don't rule out that Russia could become a member of NATO over the next two decades."[17]

Reactions to these ideas in Western Europe have been scarce. Apparently, such thoughts are still far from people's minds. Western public opinion will have to adjust considerably to accept the idea that the country so long regarded as a possible enemy may join the Western defensive alliance. Yet Clinton's words in Aachen received special applause from the audience.

OSCE

The OSCE grew out of the Conference on Security and Cooperation in Europe (CSCE). Beginning in Helsinki on June 8, 1973, the CSCE produced the Final Act, signed by thirty-five heads of state and government in Helsinki on August 1, 1975. The Soviet Union, the other states of Eastern and Central Europe, and all NATO member-states subscribed to the Final Act, which provided for regular follow-on conferences. At a CSCE summit in Paris in 1990, a Charter for a New Europe was signed, which signaled the end of the Cold War. It provided the CSCE with a permanent secretariat, intentionally set up as a small organization so as not to make it a competitor with NATO. Since then, however, the OSCE has become much larger. It has undertaken tasks— in particular through its field operations during the conflicts in the former Yugoslavia—that have gone much further than was intended, or indeed seemed necessary, in 1990. At the OSCE summit held in Istanbul on November 18–19, 1999, the expanded scope of OSCE was enshrined in a Charter for European Security, signed by the participants. This new charter, while confirming the one that had been signed in Paris nine years earlier, states that "it has become more obvious since then that threats to European security can stem from conflicts within States as well as from conflicts between States." Therefore it will "strengthen existing instruments and develop new ones."[18]

Those new instruments include

- ❖ a Platform for Co-operative Security to strengthen cooperation between the OSCE and other international organizations and institutions and provide a coordinating framework for peacekeeping efforts;

- ❖ Rapid Expert Assistance and Co-operation Teams to enable the OSCE to deploy rapidly civilian and police expertise and to answer demands for assistance in conflict prevention, crisis management, and postconflict rehabilitation;

- ❖ an Operations Center to plan and deploy OSCE forces; and

- ❖ a Preparatory Committee to strengthen the consultation process within the OSCE.

Clearly, the OSCE intends to further expand and strengthen its activities in the security field. The Istanbul document underlines that the OSCE is

- ❖ a regional arrangement under Chapter VIII of the UN Charter;

- ❖ a primary organization for the peaceful settlement of disputes within its region;

- ❖ a key instrument for early warning, conflict prevention, crisis management, and postconflict rehabilitation; and

- ❖ the inclusive and comprehensive organization for consultation, decision making, and cooperation in its region.

It even goes so far as to state that "the security of each participating state is inseparably linked to that of all others." The resemblance to the first sentence of Article 5 of the North Atlantic Treaty is striking

(Article 5 reads: "Parties agree that an armed attack against one or more of them will be considered an attack against all of them").

Some of the charter's statements seem rather overblown. The OSCE is not strong enough to fulfill all these claims and clearly is not the "comprehensive organization for decision-making in its region." Furthermore, it seems highly doubtful that the people of the Netherlands, for example, feel that their security is "inseparably linked" with that of, for example, Tajikistan, or vice versa.

This does not diminish the value of what has already been achieved by OSCE. Activities in areas such as arms limitation and confidence building, dispatching observer missions to areas of tension, and defusing ethnic conflicts through interventions by the OSCE's High Commissioner for National Minorities have achieved significant results. In addition, the OSCE has acted in its capacity of a regional organization of the United Nations as a coordinator for initiatives undertaken by other organizations or groups of states, as expressed in the Istanbul Charter. For instance, it is under the OSCE's umbrella that the stability pact for Southeastern Europe, initiated by the European Union, has finally been placed. This pact, which coincides clearly with the idea of a security community, is to be put into effect through a procedure inspired by the CSCE/OSCE tradition: three "tables" are devoted to democracy and human rights, economy and reconstruction, and security. A regional "table" covering the whole process should in principle guarantee more or less parallel progress in the three fields. Judging from the number of countries that have shown interest in participating, in one or another capacity, in this pact, the undertaking appears to be working.

THE COUNCIL OF EUROPE

The Council of Europe was founded in 1949 and is located in Strasbourg, France. It now has forty-one European member-states, including Russia. The United States and Canada do not belong. The council's numerous areas of activity include human rights, media, legal cooperation, social and economic matters, health, education, culture, heritage, sport, youth, local democracy and transfrontier cooperation, the environment, and regional planning. The council has become a focal point for discussion on human rights and legal practices. It has established the European Court in Strasbourg, which deals with human rights cases. Private citizens can bring complaints regarding human rights violations before this court against governments of member-states, including their own.

WEU

The WEU is the oldest defense organization in Europe, founded by a treaty signed on March 17, 1948. It has fulfilled some practical tasks but has usually led a marginal existence next to NATO. Only since the Maastricht Treaty opened up the possibility for requests to the WEU "to implement decisions of the Union which have defense implications" has the WEU undertaken any operational tasks. The WEU headquarters was moved from London to Brussels in 1993. It disposed of appropriate military staff, a satellite center, and a study institute. The WEU now has twenty-eight members and associate members. The associate members belong to NATO but not to the European Union. The high representative of the European Union, Javier Solana, was also named secretary general of the WEU.

The WEU's treaty contains a stronger mutual defense guarantee (Article V) than does the North Atlantic Treaty, and its assembly has more formal status and competencies than does the North Atlantic Assembly. All these facts made it difficult to incorporate the WEU into the European Union's common defense organization, as seemed desirable to the EU members of the WEU. In a meeting of WEU defense ministers on November 18, 2000, it was decided to transfer the most important of the remaining WEU institutions to the European Union, in particular the satellite center and the Institute for Security Studies. According to the decision non-EU members of WEU will remain "involved" in the activities of these institutions. Two tasks that the WEU was still performing in the Balkans were terminated during 2001. A skeleton WEU staff will stay on in Brussels to maintain the contacts with the WEU assembly and to keep Article V alive.[19] The decision of the November 2000 meeting makes it clear

that the WEU as such will play no further role in the security of the
Euroatlantic area.

WESTERN LEADERSHIP

The end of the Cold War has given Europe, Russia, and North America
an opportunity to create a system that might, over time, help the nations participating in it achieve a stable peace. But will the European
Union be able to take initiatives toward that goal?

At first glance, this seems unlikely. The difficulties facing the European leaders in formulating a common foreign policy have been set
out. The antithesis between those who see the limitation of U.S. influence as the main reason for European unification and those who
believe that a unified Europe should enhance its close links with the
North American continent is still there. Moreover, European leaders
will have their hands full with the enlargement of the European Union
and the internal reorganization this makes necessary.

Yet it is clear, as has been remarked before, that no issue would be
a better test of the European will to produce a common foreign policy than that of the relationship with North America. Member-states,
rather than squabble over policy toward North Africa or the Middle
East, should turn toward the Euroatlantic area. In fact, a common European foreign policy in general cannot really be formulated until the
relationship between the two continents has been defined. Thus, an
opportunity exists to do two things at once: to lay the basis for a stable
peace within the Euroatlantic area and to formulate a common European foreign policy.

At the beginning of the twenty-first century, relations between
Europe (and Canada) and the United States were far from optimal.
After the end of the Cold War, many observers predicted that the
United States would turn away from Europe, either to concentrate
more on Asia and the Pacific or to withdraw into the isolationism that
characterized the era after World War I. Under President Clinton that
did not happen. The uneasiness often felt by the European allies and
Canada was caused by the fact that they perceive the United States
to be exercising its monopoly as the only remaining superpower in a

unilateral way. U.S. trade policies, often pursued in an overly aggressive way, could still be considered an exuberant promotion of U.S. interests. However, decisions such as the rejection of the nuclear test ban treaty by the Senate, the failure of the U.S. administration to sign the treaty on the use of land mines, and the refusal to introduce for ratification the treaty to set up an international criminal court frightened many Europeans. It seemed that the United States was not only throwing its weight around but also disregarding the world community and the international order that it had done so much to promote.

The European uneasiness toward U.S. policy translated into statements by European leaders and former leaders that were not helpful, to say the least. The French foreign minister, Hubert Védrine, stated that common European defense forces were meant to counter the American "hyperpower." Former French president Valéry Giscard d'Estaing and former German chancellor Helmut Schmidt have written about "those in Washington who aspire to maintain some control over Europe in order to facilitate America's global political aims—and, sometimes, illusions."[20] Those statements may be inspired by a genuine feeling that some U.S. leaders are no longer concerned with the results of their actions for the rest of the world, and that the United States is no longer interested in fighting for universal values, as it has always done in the past. They may also reflect frustration with Europe's own deficiencies in defense and the lack of a coherent European foreign policy. But such statements are not the way to improve the transatlantic relationship.

The attitude of some European countries toward global U.S. foreign policy goals has not always been helpful either. Sanctions against rogue states time and again have been broken or at least circumvented by members of the European Union and by Russia. A long-term commitment to transatlantic partnership too often seems to give way to short-term commercial interests or even to a tendency to oppose the United States no matter what the reason. The United States, for its part, too often seems to assume automatic European approval of U.S. global aims that may not be shared in Europe.

The beginning of the Bush administration only increased the European unease. The new president seemed bent on reinforcing the unilateralist tendencies of the previous administration by rejecting undertakings of his predecessor. To put the UN Framework Convention on Climate Change (signed by the United States in 1992 under President George Bush) into practice, a protocol was agreed to in the Japanese city of Kyoto in 1997. This protocol may have put a burden on the U.S. economy that the new administration considered too onerous, but that it was rejected out of hand—and without warning, let alone consulting with, other nations—was a shock for all signatories. The change in policy regarding North Korea hit the South Korean government equally hard and again came without warning.

The question of missile defense is a special issue. The United States' NATO Allies and Russia and Japan would have preferred that President Bush first consult with them. However, Bush made a firm commitment to develop a missile defense system during his election campaign and thus his decision to do so was no surprise. His speech of May 1, 2001, introducing this decision showed sensitivity to Allied and Russian concerns. The teams of experts he then sent to the European allies, Japan, India, Russia, and other countries were welcomed, even though they did not relieve all anxieties, especially in Russia. Developing and deploying a missile defense system almost certainly will mean abolishing the ABM Treaty, for so long a cornerstone of nuclear arms control, in its present form. Fears have been expressed by NATO Allies as well as by Russians that a new arms race will be set in motion. Sending out these teams was a good beginning. It will remain essential for the maintenance of good U.S. relations with its allies, and with Russia as well, that U.S. authorities continue extensive consultations and listen carefully.

Meanwhile, in May 2001, some European countries very unwisely collaborated in Geneva to "bump off" U.S. representatives from the UN Committee on Human Rights and the UN Committee on Narcotic Drugs. It was, in the words of the *Economist,* "an episode that did credit to no one"[21] and undoubtedly harmed Euroatlantic relations.

Still, the situation should not be overdramatized. Relations within the Alliance have been at a low ebb before, but the tide has always turned. The conviction that Europeans and Americans have too much in common to go it alone is still strong on both sides. Opinion polls, for instance, show that a substantial majority of the population both in Europe and in North America favors continued involvement of the United States in European security affairs. There is a feeling that strongly held beliefs and vital interests continue to be shared. During his presidential campaign George W. Bush called for humility in foreign policy. President Putin has said that he wants to discuss missile defense in a spirit of partnership. Support for the NATO Alliance remains high in all member-states. But the uneasiness does point to an urgent need for farsighted leadership on both sides.

The deterioration of the relationship between the West and Russia, caused by Russian anger at NATO's action against the former Yugoslavia over Kosovo during 1999, looked even more serious. But this nadir, too, has been temporary. It can be hoped that wiser counsels will continue to prevail, that the West will more closely involve the Russians in European policy discussions, and that Russia will realize that if it wants to belong to the Euroatlantic community (as its own interests dictate) it must do a better job of guaranteeing respect for human rights within its own territory.

President Putin seems to have started trying to combine, as he has stated, democratic values with Russian traditions. Actions by his security forces against independent media have, however, caused anxiety in the West. Violations of human rights in Chechnya are still glaring, yet the Russian public does not seem prepared to lose its freedom of expression nor its press freedom. Courageous Russian nongovernmental organizations continue to criticize the government and signal human rights violations. The Russian judiciary is acting more independently and the body of civil laws is being gradually expanded. The West will have to watch further developments in Russia with an open, albeit critical, mind.

From a European perspective it would be helpful if the Bush administration, having begun the process of setting forth the basic parameters for U.S. policy toward the European Union and Russia during the president's trip to Europe in June 2001, could develop that policy further and then stick to a clear long-term policy. And frequent consultations should be continued with both. What Europeans most dislike are high-sounding phrases in presidential speeches that are not followed up by concrete actions, or presidential signatures under communiqués or charters that are then conveniently forgotten by a successor.

The enlargement of the European Union will unfortunately increase the tendency among the larger member-states to form small groups, or directorates, to precook decisions. For its part, the United States may find it expedient to test its ideas in bilateral talks with the larger EU member-states. It is logical to think that larger entities exercise a greater influence in foreign policy than smaller ones. But a stable peace can be developed only by engaging in close discussions between all the states of the Euroatlantic area, by listening to one another, by accepting contrary arguments, and by drawing conclusions jointly.

Concluding Remarks

The expansion of the European Union unfortunately causes so many institutional problems within the Union and requires so much attention from the political leadership in Europe that dramatic initiatives toward a stable peace can hardly be expected from the Union in the near future. Moreover, both North America and Russia will have to reckon with a Europe that cannot yet speak with one voice. Endeavors to create such a single voice for the Union remain unlikely to succeed as long as each country continues to follow its own foreign policy. The efforts to create a common defense force, for the time being, create more illusions than concrete results and, if not very carefully handled, may threaten to divide Europe from North America and split the Atlantic Alliance. At the same time, the debate on the future of Europe has been reopened and may lead to a better insight into the final direction European unification should take. If internal dissension can be overcome, the Union will be able to focus on cooperating more closely with North America and on coordinating American and European policies toward Russia.

In chapter 1 we stated that norms, rules, and structures can be imprinted on an international system, even before a stable peace has been achieved. The expansion of the European Union will certainly spur this process of imprinting in Central Europe, even if it takes longer than now foreseen. The relationship between North America, the European Union, and Russia can be improved immediately in certain areas, as this chapter has shown, provided that continuous attention is paid to it. Of the existing European multilateral organizations, the OSCE and the Council of Europe can in their own fields contribute to the emergence of a stable peace. NATO will ultimately prove to be the institution best suited to involving Russia in deliberations regarding European security, including peacekeeping operations.

In chapters 5 and 6 we offer recommendations for concrete policies and actions to imprint new norms and rules on Euroatlantic relations, and to improve their structure.

Another View from Europe

BY YVES PAGNIEZ

TODAY, A STABLE PEACE IN WESTERN EUROPE has fulfilled the hopes of those who started the process of reconciliation between France and Germany half a century ago.* In all European nations, the idea of Europe is at the center of their preoccupations. The European Union has become a major factor in stability on the continent, as it has become a zone of stable peace. Naturally, important issues related to the Union's future remain. Three of these are particularly significant for the purpose of this study:

- ❖ the progressive elaboration of a common European foreign and security policy;
- ❖ institutional advances within the Union;
- ❖ preparations for the entry of a dozen new members and relations with other nations.

COMMON FOREIGN POLICY

The preceding chapter pointed out that a common foreign policy does not yet exist. But we should also reflect on the significant results that have been achieved by coordination among the fifteen member-states of the Union. These range from the success of the Helsinki process (CSCE) in the 1970s, made possible by political cooperation among the member-states, to the actions taken by the fifteen during the crisis in the former Yugoslavia. Still, a gap exists between the ambitious goals set not so long ago and public perceptions of how these goals have been implemented.

---

* This commentary by Ambassador Yves Pagniez is an expression of his own views, shaped by his experiences and observations as a senior French diplomat.

The French minister of foreign affairs in early 2000 had occasion to remark on this perceived gap.[1] He observed that different words were used to describe projects launched in the fields of European finance, on the one hand, and European foreign policy, on the other—a "unique" currency but a "common" foreign policy—a difference that underscores the dissimilar conceptual approaches toward finance and foreign policy. A common foreign policy does not require the disappearance of national policies overnight but, rather, their progressive convergence over time. Through this process, the historical, cultural, and geographical specificity of each European state will be preserved as much as it can be. To suddenly replace European diversity with the lowest common denominator would represent a loss, especially in the capacity for policy innovation. A more realistic approach has the merit of limiting expectations that could not be fulfilled in the near future, the failure of which would be a source of disillusionment. This approach also will stimulate renewed efforts at coordination of foreign policy among the fifteen, especially in the domains where the Union could have its most positive role.

DEFENSE POLICY

Progress in the field of defense cooperation should not be dependent on the elaboration of an all-encompassing foreign and defense policy. The role that the European Union can play in preserving stability in the extended European system is clearly linked to the Union's capacity for crisis management, including peacekeeping and peace enforcing. The Kosovo crisis made this clear for all the governments of the member-states. It happened at the moment when Franco-British rapprochement, resulting from a French move toward NATO and a British move toward Europe, had reintroduced a certain degree of flexibility in the debate over European defense and opened the way to the decisions taken in Cologne and Helsinki, later confirmed in Nice.[2]

The goal of being able, from 2003, to project abroad, within two months, a force of sixty thousand men and to support this force's deployment for a year should be within the reach of a group of countries like the fifteen members of the Union. The pledges made at the end of 2000 for the creation of the force appear to confirm that capacity. Of course, not all the organizational and technical problems have been solved; the preceding chapter alluded to some of them.

❖ The organizational problems concern the nature and dimension of the apparatus needed to implement the new responsibilities within the Union. The Council of the Union will have at its disposal the political and security committee, a military committee, and a general staff. This improved structure will benefit from the resources released by the withering away of the WEU.[3] The Helsinki communiqué stated that the process of developing EU capacities along these lines will avoid "unnecessary duplications" with NATO. Given the different purposes of the two organizations (the Union has no intention of creating a European army), a rivalry between NATO and the European project would be senseless; their relations should develop on the basis of complementarity. The entire question, therefore, is what support the council would need for preparation and implementation of its decisions in the military field. At Nice, it was stressed that the Union should have "an autonomous capacity for decision and action in the field of defense," which implies that the European Union should be able to implement the so-called Petersberg tasks with or without cooperation from the Alliance.[4]

❖ The technical problems are linked to shortcomings, notably in air transport and communications, in the equipment of the European forces. To correct these, a financial effort will be necessary, as will close cooperation among the member-states of the Union, to produce or acquire the necessary equipment. The resulting improvement in the Europeans' military capacities, incidentally, will make their cooperation with NATO more effective.

INTERNAL REFORM

Another item at the top of the Union's agenda is the question of the improvements needed in its internal structure and procedures. Many members have stressed for a long time the necessity of improving the decision-making process before opening the door to enlargement. The results of the Nice meeting fell short of expectations and the risk still exists of a loss of momentum in the building of Europe after enlargement. The awareness of such a risk drew attention once again to the possibility of strengthened cooperation among a limited group of member-states on a particular subject. The Nice decisions made it easier for such cooperation to take place—and to do so without seeming to create a tightly knit "hard core" from which others—new members, for example—would feel excluded. Defense has been ruled out as a subject for such strengthened cooperation; progress in that area can be made only by the Union as a whole.

ENLARGEMENT AND RELATIONS WITH OTHER NATIONS

The contribution the European Union can make to stability within and around Europe depends naturally also on the relations it develops with its neighbors, with its main partners in the world, and with international organizations. One of the problems the Union may encounter in relations with its neighbors, some of them being interested in joining the European Union, is where to place the limits on extension of the Union. Widening its membership may enlarge the area of the Union's stabilizing influence but dilute its capacity for action. The basic criteria for membership of the Union are that a state be European, be democratic, and honor human rights. Naturally, new members should have settled any disputes that they may have among them-selves before they enter the Union. Beyond the borders of the Union, strategic partnerships could be established with countries that express an interest in doing so.

The main interlocutors of the Union are clearly the United States and Russia, which have been described above as involved in a tripolar relationship with the European Union. A few remarks should be added to the observations made in chapter 3 regarding transatlantic relations, the basic points of which are simple. With the United States, friend and ally, the dialogue should be a permanent one on all important subjects—for instance, European defense—to make sure that no old misunderstandings persist and no new ones develop. Dialogue does not imply accepting all arguments on either side: one should be able to say yes or no, depending on one's interests. This approach implies that discussions will proceed on a case-by-case basis. It is clear that the opinion of the different member-states of the Union may not always coincide during the course of such transatlantic discussions, but such divergences will be reconciled in the normal way within the Union.

As regards Russia, dialogue is of the essence. Today there is general agreement among Europeans as to the importance of encouraging Russia in its efforts to consolidate democracy and the rule of law. The idea of dialogue does not, of course, exempt either interlocutor from criticism; thus, for instance, there is no reason why the Union should not criticize Russia for its conduct of operations in Chechnya. To the contrary, such criticism is one way by which the members of the Union may contribute to the harmonious development of that huge land.

Finally, the building of a stable peace in Europe cannot be isolated from the situation in certain other regions. A cooperative program has been launched with the southern littoral of the Mediterranean through the "Barcelona process."[5] The European Union has for a long time shown its interest in a peaceful settlement of the Middle East crisis. It has also tried through direct aid, as well as through the Lomé agreements, to contribute to the economic and political development of the African countries.[6]

All these actions illustrate the stabilizing role the European Union can play in Europe and around its periphery in keeping with its métier as a force for peace. This is a strong group of countries, prepared to cooperate in aiding the development of the less-developed states, helping to create conditions for the progress of democracy but also prepared to act, in case of crisis, in accordance with decisions of the UN Security Council.

4

An American
Perspective

OR NEARLY HALF A CENTURY, U.S. foreign policy was inspired by
one organizing principle—containment of the Soviet Union. The
principle satisfied two basic requirements of any successful
U.S. foreign policy: it could be cast in moral terms and it seemed to
be a realistic response to U.S. strategic needs. In this chapter, we ask
whether the pursuit of a stable peace in Europe could win similar
support in the twenty-first century as a main organizing principle for
U.S. foreign policy. Is it conceivable that political leaders in the United
States would adopt this, or any other strategic paradigm, with the same
persistence and single-mindedness they have shown at times when
the nation has felt threatened by implacable enemies? Would it fit
with the moral attitudes the American people bring to foreign policy?
Would it seem to satisfy U.S. strategic concerns in the decades to
come and be supportive of the fight against terrorism? The previous
two chapters sought to answer similar questions—but, of course,
from different vantage points—concerning the feasibility of a stable
peace in Europe, both as a goal and as a guiding principle of policy.
In the next chapter we integrate our conclusions into a set of broad
policy themes.

THE CLINTON LEGACY

The main foreign policy legacy of the Clinton administration was a deep and unwavering commitment to the idea of globalization. The former president spoke of it often, both formally and extemporaneously, voicing the hope that global interdependence would make wars less likely. He talked about "the inexorable logic of globalization —that everything, from the strength of our economy to the safety of our cities, to the health of our people, depends on events not only within our borders but half a world away."[1] In his last State of the Union address, in January 2000, he called globalization "the central reality of our time."

If the Clinton administration had a grand strategy, it was the promotion of a global economy and of full and unfettered U.S. integration into it. To a large extent, his policy prescription was in tune with peculiar American strengths, but a backlash to globalization was growing even while President Clinton was presiding over U.S. foreign economic policy. Toward the end of his administration, in response to pressure from trade unions and environmental groups, he began to mention labor and environmental standards. A trade agreement with Jordan in the fall of 2000 was the first to include references to those elements. But the Clinton administration did not proceed very far down that road.

President Clinton gained approval for a North American Free Trade Area (NAFTA) but he rarely focused in his public remarks on the deeper integration of transatlantic economic relations. There were irritating trade disagreements between the United States and the European Union during his term of office that were unresolved when he left. A second major element of the Clinton legacy was a policy that embraced the idea of a peaceful, undivided, and democratic Europe, a different way of describing former president George Bush's vision of a "Europe whole and free." Clinton appeared to share the Kantian judgment, as did President Ronald Reagan and many U.S. political leaders over the years, that democracies tend not to make war upon one another. Clinton also accepted the thesis that interdependence promotes peace and that a security community must be based upon common values: "a community that upholds common standards of human rights, where people have the confidence and security to invest in the future, where nations cooperate to make war unthinkable."[2] The Clinton administration selected NATO as its chief institutional device for promoting a peaceful, undivided, and democratic Europe. Critics have argued that this caused still more division in Europe, but Clinton consistently talked about a partnership between NATO and Russia and an open-door policy for NATO membership, not excluding Russia. In his Aachen speech of June 2, 2000, Clinton defined his view of Europe: "different peoples who embrace a common destiny, play by the same rules, and affirm the same truths—that ethnic and religious hatred are unacceptable; that human rights are inalienable and universal; that differences are a source of strength, not weakness; that conflicts must be resolved by arguments, not by arms." Is the United States a part of that Europe? Yes, he suggested, because "Europe is an idea as much as a place."[3] Such was the policy of the Clinton administration. But in 2001, a peaceful, undivided, and democratic Europe may be no closer than it was in 1993.

POLICIES OF THE BUSH ADMINISTRATION

Foreign policy, as usual, did not figure significantly in the U.S. elections of 2000. George W. Bush came to office with only a set of general themes to foreshadow his policies toward Europe and Eurasia. These themes included the idea that big-power relations should be given more emphasis and "nation building" less. The implication was that Washington, in the Bush administration, would be even more reluctant than Clinton initially was to involve U.S. military forces in the Balkans. Indeed, there was a suggestion that U.S. forces would be withdrawn from the Balkans, leaving the residual job of peacekeeping to the NATO Allies. Candidate Bush's emphasis was on the Western Hemisphere. Relations with Mexico and a free trade area of the Americas would be important pillars of a Bush foreign policy.

Once in office, President Bush took steps to mark a break with the policies of President Clinton. He announced that the United States would not ratify the Kyoto Protocol on global warming and that the

U.S. dialogue with North Korea would be interrupted. He was cool toward the idea of an early meeting with President Putin. From the Pentagon came hints that the United States would concentrate more of its attention on Asia, less on Europe. On nuclear issues, Bush had made clear in the campaign that he was not inclined to support the nuclear test ban treaty and that he would proceed vigorously to create a national defense against ballistic missiles even if it meant abrogating the 1972 U.S.-Soviet/Russian treaty that precluded that.

Bush's foreign policy toward the Euroatlantic community came into focus during May and June 2001. The first step was his speech of May 1, 2001, at the National Defense University in Washington, D.C. He advocated "a new framework for security and stability that reflects the world of today."[4] Central to this was his view that ballistic missile defense should be deployed to deal with new threats from rogue states. The speech emphasized international cooperation, not unilateral U.S. actions. The speech was soon followed by signals from the White House that the administration intended to engage Russia in a search for a new framework for strategic nuclear relations.

Traveling to Europe in mid-June Bush met with skeptical NATO leaders in Brussels to outline his ideas on missile defense. French and German leaders made clear they were unconvinced. Bush's next meeting, in Stockholm with leaders of the European Union (the European Council), was noteworthy for disagreement between the United States and the European Union on the Kyoto Protocol (see discussion in chapter 3). Bush agreed that global warming was a danger but disagreed regarding ways and means to combat it.

Bush set out his policies on NATO and Russia in a speech in Warsaw on June 15, 2001. The essence of it was that he favored expanding NATO up to the borders of Russia but wanted a relationship with Russia that would make Russia firmly a part of Europe. Like other U.S. presidents—including his father—he spoke of a Europe whole and free and, like other U.S. presidents, he affirmed the fundamental role of a common value system within Europe: "the source of European unity . . . is the unity of values." He welcomed a greater role for the European Union in European security, "properly integrated with NATO." He said that "Europe's great institutions—NATO and the

European Union—can and should build partnerships with Russia and with all the countries that have emerged from the wreckage of the former Soviet Union."[5] The enlargement of NATO that Bush envisages will almost certainly alter the Alliance from a tightly linked collective defense organization to a more loosely structured collective security organization, a change that already has made itself felt.

On June 16, 2001, Bush met with Putin in Slovenia. In a joint press conference, the two presidents announced that they had agreed to launch an extensive high-level dialogue on economic and security issues. Perhaps most importantly, they agreed that their foreign and defense ministers should discuss a new security framework, "a new architecture of security in the world," as Putin called that part of the U.S.-Russia dialogue. And Putin remarked that the two sides would "discuss very specific questions which cause concern to both sides— very specific items." Bush declared himself convinced that Russia "can be a strong partner and friend, more so than people could imagine."[6]

Differences remained between the United States and the European Union and between the United States and Russia after these discussions. Few details were presented by the U.S. president regarding one of the most critical issues, ballistic missile defense. Putin made it clear that the 1972 treaty banning large-scale ballistic missile defense was important to Russia. Once back in Moscow, he declared that Russia would deploy multiwarhead missiles in response to a U.S. unilateral deployment of ballistic missile defense. The START I and II treaties, and possibly the Intermediate Range Nuclear Forces Treaty, would be rendered null and void. Putin played down the issue of NATO expansion, while making it clear that being excluded from NATO while NATO expanded to include all other European nations did not sit well with Russians.

Continuity with previous U.S. administrations is clear in President Bush's statement that Russia should be "closely bound to the rest of Europe" and that "Europe's great institutions—NATO and the European Union—can and should build partnerships with Russia." But, of course, it remains to be seen how the Bush administration's policy toward a Europe whole and free will develop as it confronts changing circumstances, including its attitude toward Russia's relationship with

Western institutions such as NATO. Equally uncertain at this writing is how the Bush team eventually will deal with the Balkans. It seems to have adopted a policy toward the Balkans more attuned to European sensibilities: "we went in together and we will come out leave together," said U.S. secretary of state Powell and President Bush.[7] Kosovo drove Russia and the West apart, but integration of Southeastern Europe into the Western economies would remove one of the historic sources of conflict between Russia and the West. The Bush administration now has the opportunity there, as elsewhere, of working for a Europe whole and free.

The Continuity of U.S.-EU Relations

Despite changes in administrations, the United States has supported European integration since the days of Jean Monnet. The post–World War II history of U.S.–Western European relations is replete with proposals for closer relations among these old democracies, including federal union. None of these ideas went very far, but the historical and cultural connections between the New World and the Old did not discourage that kind of thinking. Polls show that Americans are more positive toward political and economic unification of Europe than are some European nations and that Americans favor joint U.S.-EU decision making.[8] A more equal relationship between the European Union and the United States is generally seen as desirable and is not thought of as a zero-sum game: both parties are expected to be winners. There are, of course, differences about trade issues, global warming, and the role of governments in globalization. There are different perspectives, as between Western Europe and the United States concerning the implementation of a European security and defense identity, even though Washington's recent attitude—including that of President Bush—has been relatively sympathetic. There are different assessments concerning the value of economic sanctions, particularly in the Middle East. There are differences about NATO's role outside Europe. Such differences need not drive a wedge between the United States and the Union. In one guise or another, they have been around for a long time and they probably always will be a feature of the transatlantic landscape.

Relations between the United States and Western Europe are currently troubled by worries about a future without a common purpose. In such a future, some analysts believe that the long-standing U.S. commitment to European integration could be weakened by irrational fears of a powerful European superstate that would be less favorably inclined toward a transatlantic partnership.[9] This ambivalence has been characteristic of U.S. policy for decades. It has been especially visible regarding a European defense force. One poll taken in the United States in 1998 showed that while 50 percent of those polled thought that a joint European military force to deal with European security problems was a good idea, 45 percent thought it was not. When the public was asked about a European military force that could operate outside Europe, over 51 percent thought it was not a good idea, while only about 44 percent thought it was.[10] The opinion that a much expanded European Union confined to economic activities would be the best outcome for the United States was explicitly advocated in an article by the former national security adviser to President Carter, Zbigniew Brzezinski: "A larger Europe will expand the range of American influence without simultaneously creating a Europe so politically integrated that it could challenge the United States on matters of geopolitical importance."[11]

There are also those Americans who believe that generational change and demographic shifts will inevitably result in a lessened U.S. interest in Europe. They argue that "U.S. foreign policy will be shaped by a more diverse group of elites whose ethnic characteristics, geographic points of reference, and professional experiences will not grant Europe pride of place."[12] Stephen Walt, the author of this remark, also assumes, as do many U.S. academics of the realist school, that the absence of a common threat means that differences in national interests within the Atlantic Alliance increasingly will come to the fore and that these will override the common interest. Joint enterprises will become more difficult to sustain. In fact, the idea that the European Union will act independently of NATO on some security

issues, and will occasionally prefer a Russian to a U.S. viewpoint, has
been described as "chilling" in the U.S. media.[13]

But there are still many Americans who believe that the European Union even more than the United States is ideally positioned to take the lead in creating a security community centered on Europe that includes Russia and North America. Could this expansive vision replace the fear of attack as an overarching idea that could unite Europe and North America? Only something like this will suffice, as chapter 3 has underscored. Old democracies will instinctively huddle together when threatened, but inspirational ideas are necessary to move them to positive action. Small steps unconnected to a larger goal will founder for lack of a sense of why they deserve priority support. The solidarity of the time-tested Western community of nations was crucial to the great successes for democracy of the twentieth century and so will it be for success in the twenty-first century. Today the question is whether the European Union can resolve its internal differences over the fundamental shape of the Union of the future.

The first decade of the twenty-first century could be an historic opportunity for the Union to take the lead on an issue of global significance. Trade and financial relations are powerful incentives that the European Union brings to the table in dealing with Russia and the United States. Security issues, including the fight against terrorism, remain central to their relations. Russia's involvement in European institutions, the handling of future peacekeeping efforts in and around Europe, ballistic missile defense, and the future of NATO and the OSCE are just a few of the areas where the European Union may shape the future of Europe.

U.S.-RUSSIAN RELATIONS: A MIX OF THE NEW AND THE OLD

In contrast to the continuity in U.S.-EU relations, Americans are still feeling their way as they view events in Russia. Chechnya, Kosovo, and the handing over of power from Milosevic to Kostunica in Belgrade were difficult passages for Russia's relations with the United States. Many American experts have taken to characterizing President Putin's policies as threatening the progress of democracy in Russia.[14] Indifference or outright hostility to human rights and to an unfettered media is one charge, the latter fueled by the Russian government's actions against a leading independent television station. Another criticism is directed against the use of the Federal Security Agency (FSB) to weaken elements of civil society, particularly nongovernmental organizations. A third complaint relates to Putin's ideas about restructuring governmental institutions, for example, by weakening the independence of regional governors. Putin's Information Security Doctrine, signed by him in September 2000, also is seen as a device for discouraging open dialogue.[15] Frustrated hopes lie behind these criticisms, because those who voice these complaints assume that democratic institutions and norms are preconditions for a stable peace in Europe.

On the other hand, some U.S. scholars have pointed out that polling data indicate that the Russian people are overwhelmingly in favor of human rights and freedoms (87 percent think that the freedom to elect the country's leaders is important). Not surprisingly, the polling shows that younger Russians and those who have benefited from the abandonment of the communist system tend to support either the current Russian political system or a Western-style democracy, a hopeful sign for the future.[16] And some U.S. observers of the Russian scene also point out that Russian nationalism does not have to be destructive—it can help muster the political will to make the transition to a market economy and a political democracy.[17]

Russia's central government clearly needed strengthening if Russia was to carry out needed, but politically difficult, reforms, including changes in taxation, legal structure, and ownership of land, not to mention reducing crime and corruption.[18] Dealing with Yeltsin's government on important issues was sometimes productive, sometimes not.[19] A stronger Russian central government could be a more reliable partner on key international issues if it manages to protect the basic freedoms of the Russian people.

Russia's involvement in the global economy will require further reforms in Russia and these should increase the likelihood that governing institutions in Russia, clearly not yet fully democratic, will become more so.

What are the chances that Russian and U.S. policies can synergistically push these nations toward a security community centered on Europe? President Bush has said that Russia and the United States "have a unique opportunity to address the true threats of the twenty-first century—together. We have a great opportunity during our tenures to cast aside the suspicions and doubts that used to plague our nations. And I'm committed to do so."[20] It is easy to find reasons why suspicions may endure. The first problem that leaps to mind is highlighted by the Chinese proverb "Same bed, different dreams"; that is, material facts and ideational motivations are not identical. U.S. policymakers see NATO expansion, the NATO war against Yugoslavia, and the plan to build a defense against a limited ballistic missile attack as measures that will expand the zone of peace, underwrite the rule of law, and enhance strategic stability. Russians see these same acts in the light of their own experience and conclude that the United States is establishing positions of strength in Eastern and Central Europe and the Balkans and creating the foundation for achieving strategic nuclear superiority. Recalling experiences of the past, during periods of Russian weakness, they equate these moves to traditional power politics.

But public attitudes toward Russia in the United States contain some good news, too. Despite setbacks for U.S.-Russian relations since the euphoric days of the early 1990s, public opinion in the United States has recognized Russia's importance and supported close cooperation with Russia. A poll taken in 1998 showed that 51 percent of the U.S. people supported admitting Russia to NATO. Over 67 percent in the 1998 poll thought that the NATO-Russia Permanent Joint Council was a good idea.[21] Polls are revealing about some other attitudes that probably influence the U.S. public's thinking about Russia. Thus, 75 percent in a poll taken in March 2000 expressed the belief that nuclear weapons in the hands of Russia would pose a serious threat to world peace.[22] This is evidence that the United States and Russia are caught in the deterrence trap. Each side has nuclear weapons, mutual deterrence is embedded in the relationship, and neither knows how to escape from the political consequences of these facts. Nonetheless, 63 percent of those polled in May 2000 thought that

Russia and the United States should continue working toward reducing the number of nuclear weapons.[23] Russia is not seen as a challenge to the United States' status as a world power. According to a poll taken in September 1999, 50 percent believe that China will pose the biggest challenge to America's world power status in the next one hundred years. Only 6 percent think that Russia will.[24] In July 1999, a poll showed that 69 percent thought that relations with Russia were either extremely important or fairly important.[25] And in May 2000, 86 percent of those polled said that what happens in Russia is either important or vitally important to the United States.[26] There is no sign of "Russia fatigue" in these numbers. In March 1999, 73 percent of the U.S. public thought that ensuring that democracy succeeds in Russia was either a priority U.S. foreign policy problem or a top-priority problem.[27] The latter data were collected during the NATO bombardment of Yugoslavia. As to the lasting effect of that conflict in the eyes of the U.S. public, another poll taken in March 1999 revealed that 66 percent believed that the disagreement with Russia and China over the bombing was just a temporary problem.[28]

Nevertheless, Kosovo and Chechnya evidently seriously damaged Russia's standing among Americans. In November 1999, a Gallup Poll showed that 58 percent of those asked held an unfavorable view of Russia. But even before Bush's meeting with Putin, there was some evidence that Americans were beginning to adopt a more favorable view of Russia than had been the case during the low point of 1999–2000. A Gallup Poll conducted in February 2001 showed that 52 percent of those polled had a favorable opinion of Russia, while 42 percent had an unfavorable view. And in a Gallup Poll taken in April 2001, of those Americans asked, 11 percent thought of Russia as an ally, while 45 percent saw Russia as friendly but not an ally.[29]

These data lend support to the thesis that an accommodationist policy on the part of the Bush administration would be understood by the American people. It is unrealistic to expect the United States to stop doing all the things that Russia objects to and vice versa. But the response to terrorist attacks suggests that, over time, Russia and the United States, with a greater sense of their mutual interests, could resolve many of the points at issue. With a more effective central

administration in Moscow, and assuming progress toward democracy, some of the difficulties that have colored the Russian people's
attitudes toward the outside world also may be eased. One of the
most important things that Russia could do is align itself with Western institutions and from there gradually build its influence.[30] Difficult though this will be, moves like this are key to integrating Russia's economy into the global economy.

Russia's foreign policy also will be a key determinant of public
and official U.S. attitudes toward working with that country. Foreign
Minister Kozyrev's pro-Western policies were superseded by Minister Primakov's policies—policies less committed to the Western connection and more inclined toward maneuvering for position in the
global arena. Putin's own foreign policies are probably a work in
progress. At this point his ideas are consistent with "selective engagement," which is aimed at focusing on selected key issues. The
model is the policy of Prince Alexander Gorchakov, Russian foreign
minister in the period after the Crimean War, and of Chinese foreign policy in the period after Deng's ascendancy, with its focus on economic
growth and a limited array of other foreign policy concerns.[31] Economic relations with the European Union and security relations with
the United States are important in such a policy. A stable peace in Europe could emerge from this if Russia were able and willing to make
the changes in its internal arrangements that would facilitate close cooperation with the Union—and with the United States—a point em-
phatically made in chapter 2. However, Moscow may be tempted to
adopt a Eurasian strategy, aligning Russia with China, India, and others in opposition to U.S. positions. This, of course, would do serious
damage to prospects for a security community centered on Europe
that would include Russia. It was noted in the United States that Putin
met with Bush in June 2001, just after signing a charter for the Shanghai Cooperation Organization, prompting comment about Putin's tri-
angular diplomacy. There is no contradiction between Putin's action
and a commitment to a Euroatlantic security community, but at some
point complete freedom to maneuver for advantage between East and
West could undermine the idea of community, no matter which country engaged in the practice.

ISOLATIONISM, UNILATERALISM, OR MULTILATERAL COOPERATION?

Observers since the early days of the republic have noted a tendency for moral judgments to prevail in matters of U.S. foreign policy. This has become deeply embedded in U.S. policymaking and is often referred to as "Wilsonianism." The result, as Henry Kissinger has noted, is a tendency "to turn foreign-policy issues into a struggle between good and evil."[32] For better or worse, U.S. idealism will influence the policy the nation adopts with respect to Russia's association with the West and will inevitably affect President Bush's policies. Issues are constantly framed in this way in the United States.

Domestic politics—especially the struggle between "unilateralists" and "multilateralists," to put it simplistically—also will influence the attitudes of the Bush administration toward a stable peace in Europe. Speaking from a "multilateralist" stance, the Clinton administration declared that neo-isolationism was rampant among its adversaries. A speech given by President Clinton's national security adviser, Samuel R. Berger, at the Council on Foreign Relations in New York on October 21, 1999, outlined five principles of the "new isolationism." Closely paraphrased, these are as follows:

❖ Reject treaties as a threat to U.S. sovereignty and continued superiority, thus encouraging a world with no rules, no verification, and no constraints.

❖ Refuse to support the institutions and arrangements through which the United States shares the responsibilities of leadership, such as the United Nations.

❖ Allow foreign wars to take their course, failing to understand that local conflicts can have global consequences.

❖ Act as though a great country must have a great adversary, thus arousing Russophobia and treating China like enemy number one.

❖ Rely solely on military defenses to protect U.S. security—a survivalist foreign policy that would build a fortified fence around the country and retreat behind it.

Berger said that this attitude "would squander our advantages, alienate our friends, diminish our credibility, betray our values and discredit our example."[33] Some critics of Berger's speech recognized that "isolationism" was not the correct way to characterize the phenomena that he described. "Unilateralism," some suggested, was a more accurate term.

If unilateralism came to be a dominant tendency in U.S. thinking, there would be little chance for the emergence of a peaceful, undivided, and democratic Europe, at least one that included the United States. Prominent U.S. commentators have made the same point many times.[34] Their opinions are representative of grassroots sentiment among the American people. Despite its growing reputation for unilateralism, the United States is a nation where ordinary people are overwhelmingly in favor of multilateral organizations and collective approaches to international problems.

This is borne out in poll after poll, and it seems to be especially clear in the case of military intervention. The Chicago Council on Foreign Relations publishes a report annually entitled "American Public Opinion and U.S. Foreign Policy." The survey published in 1999 found that 72 percent of the public thought the United States should not take action alone in responding to international crises if it does not have the support of allies. Fifty-seven percent of the public agreed that the United States should take part in UN peacekeeping forces.

U.S. scholarly research accepts, with wariness, of course, the idea that there is no inherent obstacle to the realization of a peaceful, undivided, and democratic Europe, despite the problems everyone can see. Illustrative of such scholarly findings is the work of one of the most eminent U.S. historians, Paul Schroeder, who has identified four separate but interrelated trends in international history that he believes became increasingly powerful in the latter twentieth century and have sharply altered the international system. The four trends he perceives are

1. the decline of the utility of major war;
2. the rise of the trading state;
3. a dramatic increase in international communications and the integration of these exchanges into international networks to the extent that domestic affairs cannot be isolated from them;

4. the ascendancy of liberal representative democracy as the dominant legitimate form of governance of modern states and of market-oriented capitalism as the dominant form of modern economic development.

These trends, in Schroeder's opinion, have made it possible for voluntary associations for peace to avoid or overcome the weaknesses of earlier attempts. These trends must also affect the outlook for a stable peace.[35]

The mainstream of political thinking in the United States is internationalist. Both major-party candidates for the U.S. presidency in the November 2000 election spoke in this vein. George W. Bush, in his campaign, and as president, has stressed the importance of working with other countries. After meeting with NATO heads of state and government for four hours at NATO headquarters on June 13, 2001, President Bush remarked: "I hope the notion of unilateral approach died in some people's minds here. Unilateralists don't come around the table to listen to others and to share opinion."[36] Many supporters of a conservative foreign policy share the view that the United States needs friends and allies to achieve a Europe whole and free. Writing after the fall of Yugoslav president Milosevic, Robert Kagan and William Kristol said that "the United States serves its own interests best when it wields its great power on behalf of its principles." They argued that a U.S. military presence in the Balkans is necessary to "secure what just over a decade ago seemed a far-fetched hope: a Europe whole and free."[37] After Bush's European trip in June 2001, Kagan wrote that "Bush actually has offered both Europeans and Americans a vision of a different political and strategic future. And it's not a future where the United States goes it alone."[38]

Anthony Lake, former national security adviser to President Clinton, commented on the overthrow of Milosevic in October 2000 along similar lines. A peaceful, undivided, and democratic Europe, he wrote, "may be a generation or two away, but the forces of globalization, if not the policies of governments, will some day make it real. And it is deeply in our interest."[39]

What principles may guide U.S. engagement with other nations within the extended European system? The much-analyzed U.S.

tendency to oscillate between engagement and withdrawal probably has passed into history. The United States has too much at stake to withdraw from global engagement, and the American people understand this. As suggested above, another form of strategic oscillation may have replaced the older version. The current extremes are derivative forms of realism and liberal internationalism, or realpolitik and Wilsonianism. The principles of what Berger called the "new isolationism" are really a caricature of realpolitik, that is, with little or no dependence on rules and norms and primary reliance on the use of force to keep the peace. The principles of Wilsonianism, which can be equally caricatured, can be summed up as a faith in democracy, the rule of law, and international institutions to preserve peace. When U.S. realists understand that rules and norms do matter and U.S. liberal internationalists understand that power is a major factor in international relations, a constructive balance between these two poles of U.S. thinking can be reached and serve as the foundation for imaginative and effective foreign policies.[40] There may be a tendency now, encouraged by the fact that so much power of all kinds is available to the United States, to engage with the world on realist terms, at the expense of the balance provided by Wilsonian ideas. If the United States were to do so, policies of strategic restraint and accommodation, so necessary to the idea of a security community that includes Russia, would not be possible. Instead, the hallmarks of an attenuated hegemonic approach to foreign policy would dominate U.S. policies in dealing with other nations, including those of the extended European system.

The Bush administration seems to see that the main axis of U.S. strategic interests outside the Western Hemisphere runs through Eurasia. The corollary of this thesis is that a global stable peace is primarily dependent on relations between the United States, the European Union, Russia, China, and Japan. And so the question that preoccupied multipolar Europe in the nineteenth century has posed itself again: How can the major power centers jointly or severally create a framework for advancing their own individual interests while managing their inevitable differences? Here, U.S. opinion shapers differ. Some hearken back to what European statesmen of the nineteenth century discovered: that an equilibrium based on restraint among the major powers can meet fundamental national requirements. So, today, some think that an accommodation of interests among the world's power centers based on "strategic restraint" is almost self-evidently preferable to a world resentful of U.S. unilateralism.[41] But while some Americans think that relations among major power centers have become too complex and too much influenced by nonmilitary factors to allow military calculations to dominate, many others think in realpolitik terms about the need for overwhelming military power and of a benign hegemony. Bush may not have driven a stake through the heart of unilateralism in his first trip to Europe as president but he did move decisively away from the camp of those who believe the only remaining superpower need not accommodate itself to the opinions of the rest of the world. He has moved much closer toward multilateralism since September 11, 2001.

SHOULD A STABLE PEACE BE LIMITED TO EUROPE?

The United States is deeply involved in East Asia and probably will be even more so in the future. Americans will ask: If the achievement of a stable peace in the extended European system is a goal worthy of America's best efforts, should not the same be true for the other end of Eurasia? Why not work with equal zeal for a stable peace involving China, Korea, Japan, Russia, Canada, and the United States? A stable peace in Asia, of course, is a valid and reasonable goal; national policies should be devised that would promote its realization.[42] But such policies must be geared to the fact that progress toward a stable peace in Asia has been slower than in Europe.

The relationships between Japan and the United States and between the Republic of Korea and the United States could fairly be described as a stable peace. The political cultures of all three countries are similar, and even though the three national identities are obviously distinct, democratic values are respected in all three nations. These relations, however, are the exception in East Asia. Elsewhere, peace is conditional, perhaps even precarious. Even in ROK-Japan relations, a stable peace has not been fully achieved.

Thus, the first priority in East Asia must be to consolidate a benign form of conditional peace. Much has been accomplished in Russia-China relations through ending border disputes and adopting confidence-building measures. The Shanghai forum can do useful work in stabilizing Central Asia, an interest shared by the United States. Potentially serious conflict situations remain in the areas of Taiwan and Korea. The issue of the Northern Territories/South Kuriles remains unsettled. The United States and China are at odds over a variety of issues, despite much progress in economic cooperation, and during the early months of the Bush administration the air was full of suggestions that China and the United States were heading toward a Cold War–type rivalry. Until these problems—some quite fundamental—are resolved, a stable peace in much of the region must be seen as a long-term goal, even longer than in the extended European system.

LONG-TERM STRATEGIC OBJECTIVES

The Bush administration, refreshingly, seems determined to emphasize a strategic view of foreign policy: to sift out the static of daily events in order to achieve coherence in foreign policy. This attitude is the essential foundation for constructing successful long-term policies aimed at optimizing the chances for a stable peace in Europe. One element of such a policy should be focused on the European Union and, indeed, early indications are that the Bush administration would favor a policy that would strengthen the solidarity of the Western community of nations by

❖ building a Western economy that is so strong that it is both attractive to the rest of Europe and able to absorb economies that are less competitive,

❖ ensuring that the United States remains a strong and cooperative member of the Western community, and

❖ continuing the process of building a single market and pooling sovereignties within the European Union while expanding the European Union to the east as rapidly as internal integration permits.

The Western element of a U.S. strategy for a stable peace cannot be ambivalent if such a strategy is to succeed: the strategy must encourage the rise of a distinct political and economic center of gravity in Western and Central Europe—the European Union. On this foundation, other combinations can be established, whether a U.S.-EU or U.S.-EU-Russian partnership. Such a U.S. strategy also would have a significant economic component. U.S. support for the euro as a major reserve currency in global financial markets seems already accepted in Washington, but the Bush administration should seek closer U.S.-EU economic cooperation, possibly in the form of a transatlantic free trade area. This would require a shift in the administration's priorities, which have been focused on a free trade area of the Americas.

The other, and equally important, element of a U.S. strategy for a stable peace would deal with Russia. Bush and Putin agree that they should devise a new strategic framework for U.S.-Russian relations and join forces against terrorism. The Bush administration's vision, as developed during the president's June 2001 trip to Europe, seems to embrace the following policies:

❖ transforming security relationships to create a single security space throughout the Euroatlantic region;

❖ building stronger economic relationships; and

❖ supporting in every possible way the building of democracy and constitutional liberalism in Russia, recognizing that this task will succeed or fail as a result of Russian efforts and that Russian democracy will not conform exactly to other models.

What the Bush administration seems to want for Russia may be close to what most Russians want for Russia:

❖ a sturdy democracy, buttressed by a civil society and the rule of law; and

❖ economic reform and integration into the global economy.

These are conditions that cannot be imposed from outside. For example, Russia desperately needs investment. This will never come in any significant measure from foreign governments, nor can foreign governments effectively encourage private investment unless Russia itself creates the conditions for it, including a legal framework that will protect foreign investment. When conditions are favorable, Russian capital will return and foreign capital investment will grow. But in the meantime the West can encourage Russia's association with European, transatlantic, and global economic institutions.

What the Bush administration wants *from* Russia may not correspond to what many Russians have been ready to accept:

❖ a completely new paradigm for strategic nuclear relations, in which defensive measures play a much larger part than in the past and less reliance is placed on strategic offensive forces; and

❖ NATO membership for all European democracies "from the Baltic to the Black Sea," with a "fully reformed, fully democratic" Russia "closely bound to the rest of Europe."

The dialogue that Putin and Bush launched at their meeting in June 2001 is premised on the expectation that a new framework for U.S.-Russian security relations will emerge from the logic of the circumstances both nations now face. It probably will, but not overnight and not without mutual accommodation.

Chapters 5 and 6 elaborate our views on the elements of a new framework for relations between the European Union, Russia, and the United States. We suggest common lines of policy and specific proposals both to support democratic reforms in Russia and to work out a targeted trilateral (EU, U.S., Russian) agenda that will improve the prospects for a stable peace while attacking serious problems that are affecting people's lives in the here and now.

5

Policies
for a Stable Peace

THIS CHAPTER DESCRIBES BROAD POLICIES that the European Union, Russia, and the United States should pursue in parallel in order to strengthen habits of cooperation between themselves. These policies are consistent with perspectives we have described in the preceding three chapters. Furthermore, they would lend support to underlying trends that are favorable for a stable peace and would put the three parties firmly on the road to that end. In addition to outlining these policies, we also identify areas where potential disputes could engender either cooperation or conflict both within the region and beyond.

A Security Community Centered on Europe: Internal Relations

In chapter 1, we identified five models that might describe future relations between the European Union, Russia, and the United States. The one that we prefer, and believe that all the governments concerned should work for, is the first of those models, a stable triad. We understand this to mean three distinct clusters of states—so defined by historical, cultural, and geographic factors—whose relations are

shaped by similar values and by a dense network of political and economic transactions. No one of these states would dominate the others
and an equilibrium defined by power relationships—especially military power—would not be a motivating factor within the system.

In this model, the United States would remain actively engaged
in Europe. Internal integration of the European Union and its enlargement to the east would proceed satisfactorily. Russia would become
a modern European state—a democracy with a market-oriented
economy—intimately involved in European developments. Russia
would be a part of a peaceful, undivided, and democratic Europe and
would see its identity as part of that community—which also would
include North America. The three elements would be linked to the
global economy and, of course, through trade and financial dealings
with one another.

But that vision is not the current reality. Today, a world more like
the second of the models identified in chapter 1 is what exists: within
our incipient stable triad the United States is dominant because of its
cohesion and great economic power; the European Union is also
powerful in economic terms but its foreign and security policy is far
from unified; and Russia has not yet established a solid democracy
but is working on it, while it lags seriously behind its prospective
partners economically. Russia also remains outside the Western community and many Western institutions and is torn between believing
that its fundamental interests lie in cooperating with Europe and, to
the contrary, that the West threatens its fundamental interests. This
structure is internally imbalanced, not only militarily but also in its
political and economic dimensions. This imbalance could promote
temporary, perhaps even lasting, liaisons between the two weaker elements to offset perceived hegemony by the strongest, which would
generate instabilities.

The internal characteristics of the three parties would strongly
affect the foreign policies each would pursue. Thus we must consider
how the internal features of the relevant nations—and, in the case of
the Union, its structural form, as this impinges on national or collective foreign and defense policies—would affect the outlook for a stable peace in Europe. Many of the basic conditions that would tend to

promote policies conducive to a stable peace are essentially the same in each of the countries involved:

❖ a society in which democracy and democratic means of governance have taken root;

❖ a healthy economy open to international trade;

❖ a society that is open to links with other nations and sees international cooperation as a means of contributing to its own well-being;

❖ continuing advances in technology and its application to human welfare broadly; and

❖ globalization that respects labor and environmental standards.

These conditions are not firmly in place throughout the extended European system—far from it—but our judgment is that the foundations for them have been laid. It does not require a baseless leap of faith to predict that all of these conditions could be realized in another decade or two. The first two of these conditions are usually seen as problems for Russia. Russians have successfully adopted democratic practices, however, such as transfer of power through elections, and are experimenting with democratic means of governance in such areas as separation of the executive authority from judicial authorities, creation of stable political parties, and decentralization of the federal government's power over regions. Current political debate in Russia focuses on just such issues. Russia has abandoned autarkic economic practices and seeks closer relations with Western nations and membership in international trade and financial organizations. Problems remain in Russia's economy, such as aging plants and equipment and an inadequate legal framework for foreign investment, but gross domestic product (GDP) grew by 7.6 percent in 2000.[1]

As regards openness to international cooperation, application of technology to human welfare, and globalization that pays due attention to its social effects, especially on the weakest sections of society, and to the protection of the environment, each of the nations of the extended European system is guilty to some extent of failing to meet the highest standards of behavior. But each of them aspires to these ideas as goals and, especially if compared with the years leading up to World Wars I and II, their records are not too bad.

Many other developments, however, could overwhelm the favorable tendencies that we detect:

❖ nationalist sentiments that produce hostile feelings toward other nations;

❖ economic problems that give rise to protectionist policies;

❖ regional conflicts that pit nation against nation within the extended European system;

❖ antidemocratic and other tendencies that enlarge differences in value systems;

❖ demographic or other underlying trends that leave governments little time or energy for international affairs;

❖ preoccupation with other geographic regions (in the cases of Russia and the United States) that sharply curtail involvement in Europe; and

❖ an excessive focus on internal integration (in the case of the European Union) at the expense of external relations.

This is not just an abstract list. Problems that distract and divide the nations abound: The demographic outlook in Russia is bleak. Life expectancy and birth rates are down. Total population is shrinking. Health care to correct these trends is not available to the extent necessary. Growth of GDP is expected to be lower in the next few years than in 2000. Reforms necessary to attract foreign investment are not yet in place. Tariffs are still several times higher than the average in Western countries.

A fairly benign form of nationalism is a latent factor, at least, in most of the larger nations of the extended European system. Within the European Union, this factor inhibits further integration. In the United States, it produces tendencies toward unilateralism. In Russia, it creates distrust of policies of cooperation with the West. Already, armed conflicts in the Balkans and disputes over oil pipelines in the South Caucasus have soured relations between Russia and the West.

Russia is strengthening ties with India, China, and Iran, sometimes at the expense of closer ties with the United States and the European Union. The United States, concerned by potential conflicts in the Taiwan Straits, on the Korean peninsula, and in the Middle East, is committed to a further enlargement of NATO and preoccupied with building a missile defense system, despite doubts in Western Europe and Russia. It is not at all clear that the European Union will be able to revise its internal decision-making procedures sufficiently to adjust to the enlargement of the Union. The European Union, Russia, and the United States seem to understand the requirements for building a stable peace, but they will need to do more to realize those requirements and work to minimize or eliminate characteristics that militate against the achievement of a stable peace. This is the purpose of the recommendations we make in chapter 6.

Given all these negative factors, why do we say that underlying trends are favorable toward development of stable peace in Europe? Globalization and technological developments are part of the answer. The threat of terrorism is another. But still more basic is a judgment concerning the convergence of the value systems of Russia and the West.

In view not only of Chechnya but also of a host of Russian domestic problems and some of Moscow's foreign policy moves, most people in the West have refused to regard Russia as "one of us," that is, sharing the value system of Western Europe and the United States. For a vocal minority, Russia is already a renegade country, a patron of the "rogues" or even a "rogue state" itself. In view not only of Kosovo but also of Western policies toward Russia and what is seen as a cultural and information assault by the West, many members of the Russian foreign policy and defense establishments reject the Western value system as hypocritical and predatory.

It is ironic that values have become a question mark again, several years after the collapse of communism and after Russia's public embrace of democratic values, free market values, and the principle of the rule of law as codified in its constitution. It is sad that this happens after Russia has been included in the Council of Europe and has become a member of the G8. Still, the situation here is far from hopeless. Consider the following:

❖ Despite the usually strong electoral performance of the Russian Communist Party (which is not surprising in the context of the country's excruciatingly painful socioeconomic transformation), the communist system of values has the support of less than a quarter of the Russian population.[2]

❖ Russian ultranationalism remains a real but on the whole marginal force. Russia never developed into a nation-state and therefore nationalism is inherently tempered by the legacy of imperialism—in both its tsarist and communist incarnations—with its universalist claims.

❖ As for ideas of returning to the past—for example, an attempt to annex Crimea—these are held in check by the demonstration effect of the conflicts in the Balkans, the Caucasus, and Central Asia, as well as by the steady growth of individualism, which is sapping the traditional domination of the state.

❖ Virtually all political forces in Russia, including the Communists, have accepted the principles of private property, individual freedoms, and electoral democracy; the Duma has endorsed private land ownership; and the Russian people have won the right to freely leave and return to their country.

❖ Western products, standards of consumption, and lifestyles have all had an impact on the Russian market.

It is also worth remembering that over the past half century several Western countries on both sides of the Atlantic, countries undoubtedly democratic and more economically advanced than today's Russia, were engaged in colonial and postcolonial military operations overseas (some at the same time that they were members of the Council of Europe). While this should by no means serve as an excuse for Russia, a retrospective view could help put things in a broader context.

We cannot, of course, proclaim that the emergence of shared values between Russia and the West is a sure thing. The outcome will largely depend on developments in the economic and sociopolitical areas. A wealthier, happier, and younger Russia should in principle share the same values as the West, although there is no automaticity in the process. A younger but poor and unhappy population might move in the opposite direction. There is nothing about private property per se that makes the world more peaceful. However, a successful transformation of Russia's economy, polity, and society will make Russia increasingly compatible with the West in terms of values and practices. The important thing is the dynamic—that is, the direction and pace—of Russia's ideational transformation, which, we believe, is positive.

An analysis of U.S., EU, and Russian policy documents and actual policies brings us to an interesting conclusion. There is more debate and disagreement across the Atlantic than there ever was during the Cold War, and much more conflict potential between Russia and the United States, as well as between Russia and Europe, than existed a decade ago. Yet, on closer inspection the picture is different. The area of agreement is much more solid and the issues on which there is agreement are fundamental.[3] By the standards of the Cold War confrontation, Russian-Western differences, although acute, are rather peripheral. Chechnya and Kosovo are not cases of direct (or even indirect) conflict between Russia, on the one hand, and the United States and the European Union, on the other. There are no parallels, say, with Afghanistan and Vietnam. U.S. missile defense plans have aroused concern and criticism in Europe as well as in Russia. And while the implications of those plans may be feared, even in Russia most people do not see a U.S. missile defense system as a direct threat. By no stretch of the imagination can this be compared with the Euromissile crisis of the late 1970s and 1980s. NATO enlargement remains a source of dispute, as do various economic issues. Of course, there are differences between the United States and the European Union, too, over trade and defense issues, some of which have led to bad feelings on both sides of the Atlantic.

The areas of agreement, however, are vast. We believe that the core interests of the nations of the European Union, Russia, and the United States are nonconflictual and what is conflictual is not core. On both traditional and "new agenda" security issues, from nuclear security to nuclear safety to counterterrorism, Europe, Russia, and America are essentially on the same side. The ideological conflict is over, not to be rekindled. The Russian economy, even in the modesty of its present size, is part of the global economy, guided by the same driving forces. Russia's 1998 financial crisis was accentuated by negative trends in the Asian countries, which also hit other nations. Russia has a direct interest in Western growth, and vice versa, and no Western interests will be served by another Russian crisis.

Changes that will make Russia more compatible with the West have a good chance to materialize, but only in the long run. Early enthusiasm about the pace of Russian transformation has been very counterproductive.[4] But deep pessimism is equally unhelpful. Engagement with Russia should be hardheaded and pragmatic, and much patience will be required.

PARALLEL AND COMPLEMENTARY POLICIES

Russia's Policies toward the European Union and the United States

Globalization affects Russia and the West in different ways. The Russians see their country slipping into the Third World and are afraid of the consequences. A wanderer between the West and its opponents until recently, Russia was drifting toward the status of de facto ally of those who would challenge Western preeminence. Putin may have ended that drift and thereby avoided having Russia imperial pretensions, the country could wind up on the wrong side of the new divide.

The principal goal of Russia's foreign policy should be to provide resources for the country's transformation into a functioning and growing market economy; a society at peace with itself, where the rights and freedoms of an individual are guaranteed by a democratic system of government based on the rule of law; a country fully integrated with the outside world, competitive by its standards and reasonably well protected against the various external threats and risks. This overriding goal calls for a coherent set of policies with regard to the United States and the European Union aimed at attracting large-scale Western investments to Russia, ensuring the flow of technology and know-how, and opening Western markets to Russian goods and services. Much here depends on the business climate in Russia itself, such as the degree of political stability and the nature of the country's economic policy, and on the quality of Russia's legal framework and infrastructure. The type of policies we propose, however, can be genuinely successful only with the demilitarization of Russia's relations with the West. The contradictions of living with a "good" European Union and a "bad" NATO are not only mind-boggling but also a recipe for the failure of practical policies.

If Russia wants to be a success it will help itself through the following policies:

- ❖ constructing a long-term and comprehensive partnership with the European Union, leading in the medium term to a loose association with it, and proceeding toward stronger ties further from that base;
- ❖ building a satisfactory asymmetrical relationship with the United States, based on common security and geopolitical interests (such as strategic stability, nonproliferation of weapons of mass destruction, the containment of regional conflicts, and the fight against terrorism and international crime);
- ❖ expanding its participation in the G8 group and providing constructive input in discussing global issues;
- ❖ working its way to a full membership in the WTO, and then moving on to an eventual accession to the OECD;
- ❖ seeking the broadest possible access to Western economic, financial, and technological expertise, including by a series of large-scale retraining or educational projects;
- ❖ working with the European Union and the United States to help prevent, manage, or resolve conflicts in Southeastern Europe, the Caucasus, the Middle East, and elsewhere;
- ❖ making the Russia-NATO Founding Act work; and
- ❖ reaching out to the countries of Central and Eastern Europe to construct a pattern of mutually satisfying relations with them.

U.S. Policies toward the European Union and Russia

The objectives of U.S. policies should be to deepen cooperation within the transatlantic community while also working to expand steadily those areas where Russia and the West can work together in a full and equal partnership.[5] Strengthening the links among the old democracies will enhance the well-being of the peoples of North America and the European Union and should encourage Russians to want as much integration with the West as preserving their own distinctive society will allow. U.S. interests will be served by demilitarizing relations between Russia and the West and by building political, economic, and cultural links that foster habits of cooperation. Peace in Europe depends on Russia's becoming a democratic state within the extended European system and, in the final analysis, this transformation can be accomplished only by the Russians. But even if policies pursued by the United States could have no more than a marginal influence on Russia's internal development, considering the stakes involved, the effort would be justified. U.S. policies to support those goals must include the following:

❖ establishing more harmonized trade and financial relations with the European Union;

❖ maintaining an active U.S. security role in Europe while encouraging the European Union to develop stronger peacekeeping capabilities;

❖ working closely with the European Union and Russia on global security issues such as terrorism;

❖ supporting deeper internal integration of the European Union, including the development of common security and defense policies, while encouraging expansion to the east;

❖ encouraging Russian exports and U.S. direct investment in Russia as conditions in Russia permit;

❖ transforming the security relationship with Russia so that nuclear weapons no longer dominate that relationship;

❖ working to ensure that Russia's voice in European and global affairs is heeded to the extent that differing national outlooks permit;

❖ taking actions to support Russia's economic reforms;

❖ supporting the progress of democracy in Russia;

❖ seeking to resolve regional and extraregional conflicts in ways that respect the interests of the European Union and Russia, as well as states in the regions concerned.

The European Union's Policies toward Russia and the United States

If stable peace in Europe depends on Russia's becoming a democratic state within the extended European system as well as on continued participation of the United States and Canada in Europe's security, priority within the EU common foreign and security policy (CFSP) should be given to strengthening relations with the Union's North American allies and improving those with Russia.

The European Union should

❖ maintain close relations with the United States and Canada, opposing the tendency to build its CFSP on antagonism toward U.S. "hegemony";

❖ discuss trade problems with the United States in a cooperative rather than a confrontational spirit;

❖ support the progress of democracy in Russia;

❖ seek to affiliate Russia more closely with European institutions;

❖ encourage Russian cooperation with the EU common security policy (a good start was made toward this goal at the Paris EU-Russian summit in October 2000, where it was agreed that discussions would be started on how Russia might contribute to the CFSP, including the rapid reaction force);[6]

❖ seek to resolve regional conflicts in ways that respect, insofar as possible, the interests of Russia, as well as those of states in the regions concerned (a step in this direction was also taken at the EU-Russian summit in October 2000, where the Chechnya problem was debated and addressed in a joint statement that underlined that a political solution for this problem had to be sought but that any solution had to respect Russian territorial integrity; the statement also condemned "all forms of terrorism");

❖ take coordinated actions to support Russia's economic reforms;

❖ promote investments in Russia and Russian exports to the Union, provided this creates and maintains the necessary market, financial, and legal reforms; and

❖ address global security issues, including terrorism, with the United States and Russia.

FINDING COMMON GROUND: LONG TERM AND SHORT TERM

We are not describing a "lowest common denominator" approach to creating a security community centered on Europe. Those areas of cooperation that have been enthusiastically accepted by the European Union, Russia, and the United States are not numerous and have been implemented differently by the nations involved. The European Union, Russia, and the United States favor efforts to combat terrorism and counter the proliferation of weapons of mass destruction. Until recently, different political and economic interests have resulted in different responses even to the terrorist threat. Since September 11, 2001, the nations of the extended European system have shown that they can rise above their day-to-day preoccupations. They will need to keep in mind the long-term goal that they share: a stable peace throughout the extended European system. If they take this goal seriously, the conduct of their policies should become more coherent. At this stage, small steps in a common direction are all that is possible. This process is not to be confused with cooperation for cooperation's sake.

Furthermore, where only two of the three major parties can make headway toward a security community, they should do so. Models of Euroatlantic cooperation that work can serve as magnets to attract the remaining party. Admittedly, two-sided cooperation can be seen as a threat by the third party—as in the case of programs conceived in the West to enlarge NATO while permanently excluding Russia or in the case of Russian-EU opposition to a U.S.-conceived ballistic missile defense. Closer economic ties between Russia and the European Union, or between the United States and the Union, however, would strengthen the foundations of a Euroatlantic security community. We recommend such steps, whenever and wherever they can be taken.

COOPERATION IN MANAGING REGIONAL DISPUTES____

Unless regional conflicts in Europe and elsewhere can be handled in a cooperative or at least in a nonprovocative way, tensions caused by these conflicts will disrupt progress toward a stable peace in Europe.[7] Cooperation between the European Union, Russia, and the United States in resolving regional conflicts could reinforce trends toward a stable peace in Europe. Conversely, differences over the origins, implications, and methods of addressing regional conflicts will inevitably set back cooperation in Europe. Three goals in particular are relevant to regional conflicts and clearly are shared by the European Union, Russia, and the United States:

❖ contain the proliferation of weapons of mass destruction and make their use in war less likely;

❖ manage regional conflict in a way that contributes to a predictable international order and does not undercut one another's fundamental interests; and

❖ strengthen the ability of international organizations to prevent, contain, or stop regional conflict and to provide humanitarian assistance.[8]

We believe that, whatever the specific character of regional conflicts, the European Union, Russia, and the United States should be guided by these three principles. In the following pages, we describe cases of potential conflict.

The Baltic States

History and politics are closely intertwined in the newly independent Baltic states, and emotions will run high over all kinds of issues for a very long time. The governments of Latvia, Lithuania, and Estonia see themselves as victims of Russia and seek not just ties with the West but to be a part of the West. Large ethnic Russian minorities in each of these countries and Russia's own historical memories of invasions from the West prompt Russian worries about this Baltic ambition. Russian and Western policies, as well as the policies of the Baltic states, need to balance these various concerns, something that is easier said than done, of course. The long-term answer to such problems is for Russia to evolve into a "normal" European nation.

Russia cannot claim a veto over NATO membership for the Baltic states. For the West, not accepting Estonia, Latvia, and Lithuania as NATO members would be tantamount to recognizing a Russian sphere of influence over former Soviet territories, which is unacceptable. This does not mean that the West should be oblivious to the reaction that admission of the Baltic states may arouse in Russia. But Russia should recognize that NATO is becoming more "Europeanized" and that its main operational functions have become peacekeeping and peace enforcement. In terms of promoting political and economic stability in the Baltic states, their admission to NATO should come soon after they have been admitted to the European Union. In view of the present Russian attitude toward the Union, this would be an easier sequence for Russia to accept.

Belarus

A problem because the Lukashenko regime has been swimming against the democratic tide in Europe, Belarus could be troublesome in Russian-Western relations if the domestic situation there were to evolve into large-scale repression or violence. It is in the interests of the West and Russia to see Belarus replace authoritarianism with a form of democracy and open up and reform its economy. Thus, restraint and a concern for democracy in Belarus should be the principles that guide U.S.-EU-Russian policies toward Belarus.

Ukraine

Ukraine is in peril of becoming a failed state, both economically and politically. It is the recipient of much Western economic assistance, but needed reforms have languished as the government has lurched from one political crisis to another. And yet the potential is there in resources, geography, and population to make Ukraine one of the richest and most important nations of Europe. There are those in Ukraine and elsewhere who would like to see Ukraine fully integrate into Western Europe, accept Western ways, and join Western institutions. There are those, too, who cherish Ukraine's history and contribution to Slavic culture and who value the country's strong ties with Moscow.[9] Both of these broad tendencies must be accommodated, since they reflect Ukraine's dual interests in becoming a modern European nation while cultivating economic, political, and cultural associations with Russia.

Many compromises will have to be made along the way, but the interests of Russia and the West in Ukraine, while not identical, are similar. Both want a Ukraine that is a net contributor to peace and security in Europe, not a source of instability and conflict. Cooperation to achieve this should be possible. But, as is the case with Russia, even though it benefits from external assistance, Ukraine must solve its internal problems through its own efforts. Neither external pressure nor external tutelage is appropriate. Instead, Ukraine should be given incentives, in the form of access to markets and connections to international financial institutions, and targeted economic help, for example, in meeting its energy needs. The stakes in the outcome of Ukraine's struggles are high, not least the progress of Russia and the West toward a stable peace.

The Balkans

Wars in the Balkans have shadowed European history for centuries and did so again in the last years of the twentieth century. The conflict in Macedonia in 2001 could destabilize relations between Greece, Turkey, and Bulgaria, as well as Serbia and Albania. In other times, large-scale European wars boiled up out of the Balkans. Tragic though the recent wars were in so many respects, they did not ignite a wider conflagration this time; and since the fall of Slobodan Milosevic, an opportunity has opened for EU, Russian, and U.S. cooperation in Southeastern Europe. All three parties share an interest in the consolidation of democracy and economic progress in the region. Threats to the stability of Macedonia require close cooperation between the European Union, Russia, and the United States, which will not be easy to achieve. But Russia played an important diplomatic role in settling the Kosovo conflict and may be inclined to make good use of its links to Serbia to help the transition launched by President Vojislav Kostunica. Extradition of all major war criminals in the former Yugoslavia to The Hague is one of the keys to normal relations between Yugoslavia and the West.

Chechnya

The European Union and the United States should be prepared to help rebuild Chechen society, although Chechnya probably will offer few opportunities for cooperation. Some in the West see parallels between Algeria's struggle for independence from France and Chechnya's struggle against Russian rule. The fundamental differences between the West and Russia over Chechnya, however, are not about Russia's sovereignty over Chechnya.

The basic criticism of Russia's actions in Chechnya has centered on Russia's conduct of what the Russians have officially dubbed a counterterrorist operation. Since September 11, 2001, the need for a negotiated peace has become even more evident. But Chechnya probably will remain a source of tension between Russia and the West.

Russians perceive Chechnya as a base for criminals and terrorism and worry that the unraveling of the federation might not stop with Chechen independence. It is in the interests of the Russians themselves, however, to look for ways to bring about a political settlement in Chechnya. Harsh measures that make the Chechen people suffer only make that search more difficult and the casualty list longer. And displaying leniency toward offenses against civilized behavior and toward criminals who happen to be wearing uniforms corrupts and demoralizes the armed forces.

South Caucasus

Although the South Caucasus has witnessed significant violence since the early 1990s, opportunities exist for cooperation as well as for conflict. The pipeline issue is a good example. Alternative routes for oil from the Caspian region have been discussed by governments and oil companies, but no consensus has yet emerged, partly because the states involved have perceived their interests to be competing and have sought to influence their oil companies accordingly. Multiple routes to ensure a continued oil supply to the world market are desirable. Economic and environmental considerations, not geopolitical factors, should dictate the decision as to what those routes should be. Economic pressure on Azerbaijan, Georgia, and Armenia to secure special concessions for Russia will be met with similar tactics by Western nations. Energy and debt relief should be areas for cooperation, not conflict. At the joint press conference of Presidents Bush and Putin in June 2001, Putin spoke positively about U.S.-Russian cooperation in transporting oil from the Caspian basin.[11]

The conflict between Azerbaijan and Armenia over Nagorno-Karabakh is another opportunity for cooperation. The European Union, Russia, and the United States could, and have, made common cause in seeking to resolve the conflict. Cooperation within the framework of the OSCE should be a prime objective.

Persian Gulf

The main issue for the European Union, the United States, and Russia in the Persian Gulf is how to deal with Saddam Hussein's continuing interest in acquiring weapons of mass destruction. Differences between the United States, Russia, and some members of the European Union have arisen over economic sanctions and have the potential to undermine efforts to create a Europe-centered security community. Some of these differences arise from differing perceptions of the threat posed by Saddam Hussein's pursuit of weapons of mass destruction. On the issue of sanctions against Iraq, Russia has preferred a softer approach than have others, while some U.S. officials favor support for anti-Saddam groups in Iraq.

Similar differences of opinion exist over Iran's nuclear interests. The EU nations, Russia, and the United States agree neither on Iran's intentions nor on how best to respond to developments in Iran. Putin has argued that U.S. complaints about Russia's sale of defensive arms to Iran amount to "unfair competition in the arms market" and that U.S. companies have offered Iran "large-scale" cooperation. He maintains, however, that Russia is committed to not supplying nuclear or ballistic missile technology to Iran and would try to stop any Russian entities from carrying out illicit sales to Iran.[12]

It appears that constructive dialogue with Iran may become possible in light of its changing domestic situation. This might help to bring about a greater convergence in the attitudes of the EU nations, Russia, and the United States. Tehran should be helped out of its current semi-isolation if it embraces a more responsible foreign policy. Both Russia and the West agree on this.

Central Asia

The "Great Game"—as the conduct of great-power rivalries in nineteenth-century Central Asia was known—is no longer being played in this region. Misunderstandings between Russia and the West could arise nonetheless if diplomacy on both sides fails to clarify the purposes of their policies and to reassure major potential actors that their interests in Central Asia are not being adversely affected. Frictions may arise over the oil and gas fields just east of the Caspian Sea, for example. And, of course, China may compete for influence and resources in a way that was not possible in the nineteenth century; this might also generate controversy in the region. At the same time, opportunities for cooperation between Russia and the West abound, mainly in helping to resolve conflicts and in fighting terrorism and drug trafficking.

For many Russians, militant Islam is the clear and present danger. Yet Russia must be careful. Russian attempts to posture as the forward bastion of the West against the "barbarians" will not produce the desired understanding by the West, which will look at Russia's means, not just its stated goals, and is likely to alienate the Muslim world, which includes not only Russia's neighbors to the south but also a sizable minority inside the Russian Federation. It would be best to concentrate on the root causes of Islamic militancy, which are socioeconomic and political, and to help moderate the practices of the governments responsible for the current unrest.

HUMANITARIAN INTERVENTIONS

The European Union, Russia, and the United States, working in harmony, can have an enormous impact on the strengthening of global norms. Working together they can help defeat terrorism, block the further spread of weapons of mass destruction, protect the environment, and prevent wars of aggression by one nation against another. To a great extent, the potential members of a security community centered on Europe share common views about these norms, although they have difficulties in translating agreement in principle into practical action.

There are serious differences of opinion, however, on the question of whether the international community has the right (and even the duty) to intervene in the case of a government's gross mistreatment of its own citizens. Is this to be considered an emerging norm? The answer will lie in whether the nations conclude that such a monstrous policy as "ethnic cleansing" cannot be tolerated anywhere in the world, and especially not in present-day Europe. Can governments that practice such policies against their own citizens be allowed to do so? The German government of 1999 was so moved by this question that it decided to break with the post–World War II practice of not sending Bundeswehr soldiers for combat duty abroad, and to join other NATO members in the use of military force to stop Milosevic's expulsion of the Kosovars from Kosovo. Up to the point where the use of force against Milosevic was being actively considered, Russia supported diplomatic and economic efforts to settle the Kosovo problem. However, had the UN Security Council been asked to affirm that the use of force was justified, Russia would have vetoed a resolution to that effect. When NATO air power was used to force a settlement without a new Security Council resolution Russia complained bitterly. This issue of if, when, and how to use force in defiance of the principles of sovereignty and noninterference in internal affairs continues to be a source of tension among the nations of the European Union, Russia, and the United States.

RELATIONS WITH ASIA

The place of the United States in the power structure of Asia has been fixed and predictable for decades, just as it has been in Europe. There has been no question of the United States reversing alliances or realigning itself in the region, and this will not happen in the foreseeable future, if only because the U.S. style of government and foreign policy does not lend itself to such maneuverings. Russia has resolved its border disputes with China and is developing a relationship with Beijing that it calls a "partnership." Balance-of-power considerations have played an explicit role in these developments, as have other issues, for example, ballistic missile defense, where Russia and China share similar viewpoints. The upgrading of Chinese-Russian cooperation in Central Asia was signaled by the signing of the founding charter establishing the Shanghai Cooperation Organization in June 2001.[13] Moscow understands very clearly, however, that its evolution toward becoming a "normal" European nation requires a qualitatively different set of relationships with the West. Typical of a number of Russian public statements on the matter was one made by Putin in his press conference with French president Chirac on October 30, 2000: "Both historically, in the cultural sense, and increasingly in the economic sense, too, Russia is very much part of Europe, the greater Europe."[14] Because of its geographic position, the European Union's interests in Asia are overwhelmingly economic and that is likely to remain the case.

Steadiness, not a shifting balance of power, produces equilibrium under present-day circumstances. Also needed are a method and a habit of accommodating differing national interests within a well-understood framework of restraint. This mechanism of mutual accommodation is the most that can be hoped for in Asia in the decades ahead. It would be a very positive development. A stable peace is a real possibility within an extended European system because value systems, self-identification, and historical experiences all reinforce the stabilizing trends resulting from technological developments and globalization. The same cannot be said for Asia, but as globalization proceeds, its effects probably will become so powerful that they will overcome the centrifugal effects of cultural differences —differences that will certainly persist in the future as they have for millennia. In the meantime, an entrenched form of conditional peace in Asia is a highly desirable goal, an outcome that will suit every nation's interests.

IMPLICATIONS FOR INTERNATIONAL ORGANIZATIONS

The Euroatlantic community has been engaged in institution building not unlike the efforts that followed earlier European convulsions such as the Napoleonic Wars and World War I. However, now, after the end of the Cold War, there is a significant difference. The European Union has created an entirely new political and economic structure in Western Europe. And for the first time in history Washington and Moscow are both involved in creating organizations that will link North America and all the states in Europe.

Decisions by a government require organizations to carry them out. The policies we advocate will succeed to the extent that intergovernmental organizations are available to help implement them. The European Union, of course, is central to this whole enterprise. The OSCE, the Council of Europe, and NATO also have special roles to play, as we discussed in chapter 3. In the pages that follow, we assess the roles that these organizations could play in building a stable peace.

OSCE

Can the fifty-five members of the OSCE develop it into a peacekeeping institution? The OSCE has been held up by some commentators as the central institutional pillar of a regional security regime for Europe.[15] For this reason the decision-making rules within the OSCE need to be well understood. The principle of unanimity, or at least consensus (where one or more countries are not in favor of a decision but do not oppose it), is the basic rule. A strict interpretation of this rule allows the organization to intervene in crises only when no OSCE member-state formally objects to such an initiative. An attempt was made several years ago to overcome this obstacle by introducing the possibility of making a decision despite the opposition of a state with a direct interest in the case—in a procedure called "consensus minus one." In 1992 the exclusion of Yugoslavia from the debates of the OSCE was decided that way. The idea of a "consensus minus two" was also aired at that time to take care of situations when, two different states being involved in a dispute, the organization would run the risk of being paralyzed by their refusal of any solution.

This effort to find more flexible ways of decision making has not been continued and, during the debates at the Istanbul meeting on November 18–19, 1999, of the OSCE, the emphasis was again placed on the principle of consensus. Although the possibility of making exceptions has not been completely ruled out, the tendency has been to reaffirm the sovereignty of each state. The capacity of OSCE to undertake conflict prevention or crisis management is therefore fundamentally restricted. But the OSCE can be used for conflict resolution. Long-term diplomatic missions to observe potential conflict situations and to oversee democratic elections are a critical component of a stable peace in Europe. Much more can be done to train OSCE personnel and to fund its operations, the cost of which is slight compared with peacekeeping operations.

The Council of Europe

Human rights discussions in the Council of Europe since 1999 have centered on Chechnya. Despite the acrimony that has characterized some of the discussions, including those regarding Russia's conduct in the North Caucasus, Russia's involvement with the council, and the council's with Russia, are essential for Russia's eventual transformation into a law-based society and for the council's ambition to create a pan-European legal space. The European Court in Strasbourg already has shown itself capable of correcting some of the deficiencies of national legal systems and of bringing governments to account. For many ordinary Russians, the European Court is the ultimate court of appeal. The court, and other instruments not directly related to security matters, should be used to the fullest possible extent to anchor Russia in Europe.

NATO

The fundamental problem of Russia's relations with NATO lies in the fact that neither Russia nor the Alliance is seriously contemplating full membership for Russia. The working assumption of this book, however, is that eventual Russian membership in NATO should not be excluded as a viable road toward stable peace. Neither European nor Russian security can be ensured unless NATO finds a way of realistically engaging Russia and unless Russia is able to draw real benefits from its relationship with the Alliance. The range of possible joint ventures can be fairly broad, from sharing practical experience with military reform to terrorism to addressing the future missile proliferation threat. The habit of working together in training exercises, in discussions of military doctrine, and in force planning and budgeting discussions also is an excellent way to prepare Russian and Western military forces for common tasks. Blending military units in a composite force where the "enemy" is a catastrophe inflicted on innocent people will help to break down the barriers between Russia and the West.

The Alliance is already very different from the one that served the West so well during the Cold War. It may be only one instrument for building a stable peace in Europe, yet it is probably the only organization that could bind Russia to the West while at the same time giving Russia the participation in decision making on key political and military questions that it wants and to which its size and resources in principle entitle it. Bosnia and Kosovo have shown that peace-enforcing and peacekeeping operations in Europe should not be carried out while ignoring the Russians. On the contrary, Russian participation can provide not only precedents for future cooperation and help to create a system of shared values but also a forum for discussion and resolution of conflicts. Such participation would also diminish the risk of Russia exercising a veto when peacekeeping operations are discussed in the UN Security Council.

Of course, membership would be open only to a truly democratic Russia and time must pass before membership in NATO becomes a realistic option. Democracy in Russia will, it seems, leave much to be desired for the immediate future. Whether Western public opinion accepts the idea of Russian membership will depend on its perception of progress in Russia's development of democratic institutions, as well as on the way the proposal is presented by leaders on both sides of the Atlantic.

Can NATO help create the conditions for a stable peace within the extended European system? Given its history, can NATO be a unifying force, an organization whose contribution is useful to all the nations of a prospective security community centered on Europe? Anyone who has followed the NATO enlargement debate is familiar with the rationales for affirmative answers to these questions:

❖ First, NATO creates or reinforces stability by providing reassurance to its members and by helping to resolve ethnic conflicts affecting some prospective members.

❖ Second, by doing so, NATO enhances the security of Russia and other nations of Europe; its internal practices—for example, joint military planning and multilateral commands and formations—have "denationalized" defense operations and thus fortify NATO's status as a purely defensive alliance.

❖ Third, NATO is anyway now as much a peacekeeping operation as it is a collective defense organization.

❖ Fourth, membership is open to all the states of Europe, including Russia, that meet criteria such as civilian control of the military.

But there is another side to the debate:

❖ First, NATO's underlying mission is to guard against a resurgence of imperialist tendencies in Moscow.

❖ Second, nations applying for NATO membership are doing so with Russia's history in mind, giving the whole process an anti-Russian cast.

❖ Third, Russia's interests in Europe are not likely to receive an unbiased hearing in NATO-dominated forums.

❖ Fourth, NATO enlargement moves military bases that could be used against Russia ever closer to Russia's borders.

❖ Fifth, new lines that divide Europe into opposing camps are steadily moving east, leaving Russia more isolated.

❖ Sixth, the power behind all of this is neither a European nation nor the European Union—it is the United States, which is seeking to improve its strategic position against a potential peer.

Each of these assessments is correct and each is incorrect, depending upon a particular government's intentions, which change from time to time. No wonder that perceptions are so different and that people talk past one another so often.

Objectively, it is certain that for a long time to come intrastate conflicts in Europe, humanitarian crises, and extraregional conflicts will require a Europe-based joint military structure that can deal effectively with such problems. We think that such a structure should not be perceived as being U.S.-dominated. To the contrary, we believe it should make room for each of the three players, the European Union, Russia, and the United States.

Much time will be required to put such a structure in place. While the foundations for this structure are being laid, the European Union, Russia, and the United States need to

❖ gain experience in joint military operations;

❖ address jointly issues of global concern, such as terrorism and the proliferation of weapons of mass destruction (and the means of their delivery), as well as defenses against such threats;

❖ consider together how to enhance long-term stability in Southeastern Europe; and

❖ harmonize their policies regarding all the potential regional and extraregional conflicts mentioned earlier in this chapter.

All things considered, we see no reason why NATO—or something very much like it—could not become the organizational framework for accomplishing all of the above. In fact, NATO is better positioned to take on these tasks than other existing organizations. The European Union, even assuming it fulfills its present goals, always will have a membership that excludes Russia and the United States. The OSCE will have extreme difficulty in grafting a military component onto its present structure. A new organization could be invented, but that would probably require more effort than transforming NATO, a process that already is far along. In fact, each of the four near-term tasks identified above in which the European Union, Russia, and the United States need to be involved could be undertaken within the NATO and NATO-Russia Permanent Joint Council framework as it now exists. Moreover, NATO is clearly moving toward an arrangement in which influence is more equally shared between the United States and Europe.

But more time is needed to let these processes evolve still further. There is no security threat that is so urgent that NATO must be enlarged before the processes of change have taken hold. Change can best be encouraged through economic means, although we certainly do not mean to downplay the importance of military cooperation in confronting many of Europe's problems. Therefore, we favor policies that would consolidate a climate of confidence and stability in Eastern and Southeastern Europe through efforts spearheaded by the European Union. Can the European Union, Russia, and the United States agree on a common policy along these lines, understanding that once an accommodation to the Union's system has been accomplished by nations in Eastern Europe, membership in NATO or in an organization much like it could almost certainly follow? We believe so, but we plead for time to allow this to happen.[16]

CONCLUDING REMARKS

In this chapter we have pointed to underlying social trends and to other developments such as global and regional economic integration and the continued vitality of democratic habits in Russia that we believe augur well for progress toward a stable peace. Opposing these favorable developments, however, are other, negative, trends such as an excessive preoccupation with internal matters at the expense of cooperative, internationalist policies and challenges to democratic institutions posed by xenophobic nationalism and by a desire to concentrate power in the hands of a central government. These other developments could destroy any hope that a security community centered on Europe will ultimately emerge from the present political situation, in which peace is only conditional.

We attach great weight to the contribution to a stable peace made by value systems that, while distinctively associated with particular societies, are similar enough to be thought of as common value systems. Some of the negative trends we have identified in this chapter could drive value systems apart, rather than closer together.

The concerted national strategies needed to shape a stable peace would be difficult to achieve if underlying trends were, on balance, unfavorable. Admittedly, whether trends are favorable or unfavorable is a matter of judgment. Perhaps because we tend to read the present environment in the light of where the extended European system has been in past decades and centuries, we are optimistic about its future. Furthermore, we believe that some of the same policies that would nudge the Euroatlantic community toward a stable peace would also create a beneficial internal climate, supporting social trends that we regard as favorable for a stable peace. For example, if the image of a national adversary—another state within the system—is replaced by positive examples of international cooperation in fighting terrorism, this will tend to support underlying trends that are moving value systems—including attitudes toward interstate conflict—toward greater convergence.

We cannot prove this hypothesis on the basis of currently available evidence, but events often used to highlight differences between Russia and the West also reveal discontinuities in the projection of trend lines established by historical precedents. Some would argue, for example, that the real success of external intervention in the Balkans in recent years has been that the major actors found it possible to agree on many things, and when they disagreed, did so in a way that was vastly different from historical norms.[17] Granted, this success can be traced, in part, to Russia's enfeebled condition, but credit also can be given to the fact that none of the major actors sees war with another major actor as a serious policy option. It is probably not too early to suggest that even though their basic interests, as perceived by

Russia and the West, will diverge from time to time, their approaches to regulating conflict may be converging. This is key to the emergence of a stable peace.

With these thoughts guiding our analysis, we have set out in this chapter some broad policy lines that we recommend be pursued by the European Union, Russia, and the United States. Some of these policies would affect interactions among the three main parties in ways that would have a direct impact on internal developments. We have also reviewed potential or actual disputes within the extended European system and beyond, which present opportunities for cooperation as well as conflict. In some cases, for example, on NATO enlargement, we have offered policy guidelines that emphasize cooperation and diminish the potential for conflict. Our intention in the next chapter is to offer practical suggestions for advancing step by step down the path toward stable peace. These are essentially first steps, since we do not believe that it is possible or desirable to lay out a road map identifying each step along the way in what is bound to be a very long journey. But it is not enough to proclaim a grand design and to lay out a general strategy that may, in time, with luck, lead to a stable peace. A commitment to a long-term goal must be accompanied by a set of specific policies that address today's problems, even while incrementally building the foundations for a stable peace that may be realized only after decades have passed.

6

An Agenda for a Stable Peace

I N CHAPTER 5 WE DISCUSSED general lines of policy that we believe to be compatible with the situations within the European Union, Russia, and the United States, that would reinforce positive trends within them, and that would point the way to enhanced cooperation between them. In this chapter we offer specific proposals to implement the general programs we advocated in chapter 5. The tragedy of September 11, 2001, impels us to urge that these actions should be taken in the near future to build momentum for policies that would favor a stable peace in Europe. These recommendations include actions that the United States, the European Union, and Russia should take in parallel and that will strengthen the habit of trilateral cooperation.

TRANSATLANTIC RELATIONS

1. We recommend that the Bush administration develop a comprehensive long-term policy toward NATO that addresses NATO's future peacekeeping and counterterrorism role, enlargement, and relations with nonmember states. This policy should be thoroughly discussed with the NATO Allies and changed if necessary in light of those discussions, but then should be the guide for U.S. actions in

the years ahead. It should also be discussed at an early stage with the Russians.

The fiftieth anniversary of NATO in 1999 provided an occasion to consider the long-term future of relations within the Atlantic Alliance and with Russia. The Washington Declaration, signed by the heads of state and government meeting in Washington, spoke of

- ❖ an open door—"the vital partnership between Europe and North America . . . remains open to all European democracies regardless of geography";
- ❖ a goal—"a Europe whole and free, where security and prosperity are shared and indivisible"; and
- ❖ a result—"a community of democracies . . . where war becomes unthinkable."[1]

Judging by Bush's statements during the course of his June 2001 trip to Europe, he agrees with these aspirations. But much has changed since 1999 in the European Union, in Russia, and in the United States. Policies need to be adapted, as Bush has remarked, "to the world as it is, not as it used to be." The need to adapt applies to fundamental issues, including, in Putin's words, "building a new architecture of security in the world."[2]

Bush began to outline his administration's policies toward Russia and Western Europe during his visit to Europe in June 2001. The frank talks he had with the NATO allies were a good first step toward developing a long-term policy. A more detailed and determinative presentation of the Bush administration's policy toward NATO should build on these discussions. The next few years are likely to be watershed years for the European Union and for Russia, pointing to the direction the extended European system of nations will follow for decades to come. As the principal international security organization in Europe, NATO can have an influence on this direction of travel, but piecemeal, ad hoc decisions will not suffice. A strategic vision for NATO is needed and this is what the Bush administration is uniquely positioned to provide.

Essential elements of this policy should address peacekeeping, NATO enlargement, and relations with nonmember states.

Peacekeeping

The United States should

- ❖ assist the United Nations in improving the effectiveness of its peacekeeping and peace-enforcing operations;

- ❖ make clear to what extent and on the basis of what kind of a mandate it expects support in principle from the NATO Allies for peacekeeping operations outside the NATO area, realizing that circumstances as they exist at the time decisions on such operations are made will exert a major influence; and

- ❖ discuss with its NATO Allies what kind of legitimizing authority it envisages in cases where no mandate for peace-enforcing or peacekeeping operations can be obtained from the UN Security Council.

NATO Enlargement

- ❖ The United States should coordinate the further enlargement of NATO with the European Union's enlargement process, at least implicitly as far as timing is concerned.

NATO members should not retreat from the prospect of further enlargement, but they should also consider how NATO's contribution to a stable peace can best be realized. This consideration is likely to affect the timing of future decisions to accept new members. The expansion of NATO and of the European Union are two parts of the same process: the enlargement of the Western world. Yet, Russia broadly welcomes the latter while protesting the former. In general, the best way to enlarge NATO is first to enlarge the European Union: to welcome new members into the European Union and, soon after, accept these nations into NATO. The order of accession to the two premier Western institutions can make all the difference between erasing old dividing lines and creating new ones.

Relations with Nonmember States

❖ The United States should make clear how it intends to ensure Russia's participation in Euroatlantic decision making and, whenever Russian policies conflict with Western ones, to reconcile them to the fullest extent possible.

Russia's changeover from a superpower to a normal European nation is a difficult process. Without granting Russia a veto over NATO expansion or conceding essential elements of their own policies, Western nations should show understanding for this process and for the sensitivities inherent in it.

❖ Russia and Ukraine, as well as candidates for membership in NATO, should take full advantage of the Partnership for Peace (PfP). These nations should be encouraged, by financial assistance if necessary, to participate in the PfP.

The PfP has done excellent work. It offers a mechanism for doing nearly everything that NATO membership provides. Already the PfP has improved the abilities of the participants to respond to peacekeeping requirements and doubtless it could help with counterterrorism, too.

2. We recommend that the Bush administration develop a comprehensive long-term policy toward the European Union that addresses EU enlargement, a European common defense force, the integration of the Balkans into the rest of Europe, and the improvement of economic relations.

Support for EU Enlargement

❖ While encouraging the European Union to expand to the east to enhance stability in Central and Eastern Europe, the United States should also recognize that weakening the cohesion and strength of the Union would be a threat to the stability of Europe. Enlargement requires difficult internal reforms, however, without which the cohesion and strength of the Union would be weakened. Accepting new members into the Union before its internal reforms are further advanced would be more of a setback to European security than would a delay in the inclusion of new members that may be ill prepared for admission.

Support for a Common European Defense Force

❖ The U.S. administration should support and be prepared to work with a common European defense force, as long as the European Union provides complete transparency toward NATO and avoids duplication as much as possible.

In his speech in Warsaw on June 15, 2001, Bush said that the United States would "welcome a greater role for the EU in European security, properly integrated with NATO." Much remains to be done before the European Union's rapid deployment force will be fully effective and operational. The process of forming such a force is a natural development in the context of greater European unification and could have the added benefit of reversing the downward trend of defense budgets in Europe, strengthening units that would also remain assigned to NATO, and adapting those units more fully to tasks that will be demanded from the Alliance in the future. The European common defense force should be set up and strengthened in close cooperation with NATO. It should neither detract from NATO's primary role nor duplicate its facilities more than strictly necessary. Close cooperation should be maintained with the NATO members who are not members of the European Union for the purposes of harmonizing policies. It would harm transatlantic relations if the European Union were to separate its planning for a rapid deployment force from that of NATO and not make its plans available to its Allies, or if it were to see the common defense formation mainly in a context of opposing American hegemony. The Union should also avoid unrealistic and contradictory claims that unnecessarily disrupt transatlantic relations (as described in chapter 3).

Continued Involvement in Southeastern Europe

❖ The United States should continue to work with the EU countries in providing technical and financial support for the purpose of integrating the economies of Southeastern Europe into the larger European regional economy. Serbia should receive economic assistance provided it maintains the rule of law and democracy.

A stable peace in Europe cannot be achieved unless conflicts in the Balkans can be contained and, ultimately, resolved. The task will require sustained effort for decades, as events in Bosnia, Kosovo, and Macedonia have shown. The job of trying to harmonize the interests of Russia, the European Union, and the United States in rebuilding Southeastern Europe will itself be a test of whether the political will exists to reconcile differing national views. Russia is not in a position to extend economic assistance, but Russia's support for difficult political decisions in Serbia and elsewhere will be important.

Improving Economic Relations

❖ The Bush administration evidently intends to fight against protectionist tendencies in the United States and in doing so it should use the New Transatlantic Agenda and other transatlantic channels to discuss trade disputes at expert levels before these disputes threaten the cohesion of the Euroatlantic area.

❖ An international secretariat consisting of a limited number of senior professionals based in Brussels should be established by the United States, Canada, and the European Union for the New Transatlantic Agenda. The director of the secretariat could serve for a fixed term, with the position alternating between North American and European representatives.

The building of a stable peace in Europe depends heavily on the sustained success of the transatlantic community in working cooperatively in several crucial areas. The New Transatlantic Agenda has provided a useful forum for discussions between EU and U.S. representatives. Its value would be enhanced if it were to act as a forum in permanent session with a kind of "conscience" in the form of a secretariat that would help anticipate potential problems in the areas of trade and finance. By offering recommendations to resolve issues in a timely fashion, the secretariat could help to accommodate differing views. It may also be useful in coordinating economic support for Russia.

3. We believe that the European Union, if it is to play its vital role in the creation of a stable Euroatlantic security community, should use the convening of its new intergovernmental commission in 2004 to

put its house in democratic order before the admission of new members. It would then be able to create the necessary instruments to further integrate the foreign policies of the member-states of the Union and to formulate a common strategy regarding its relations with the United States.

Internal Reform

The Belgian prime minister, Guy Verhofstadt, holding the EU presidency in the second half of 2001, has stated that the European Union risks getting bogged down or becoming diverted by conflicting national interests, thus falling into institutional disarray.[3] "In a European Union with twenty-seven Member States," he said, "intergovernmental cooperation, if it is not to lead to indecisiveness, will inevitably take the form of a 'directoire' or, in other words, a de facto administration by some larger Member States."

Such an undemocratic outcome can be avoided only by accepting the following proposals, which Verhofstadt put forward among many others:

- ❖ decisions in the European Council should normally be taken by majority vote and under the democratic control of the European Parliament;

- ❖ the European Council should eventually be transformed into a second chamber of the Parliament, a senate representing the member-states;

- ❖ the European Commission's role should be strengthened— indeed, the European Commission should eventually be transformed into a government responsible to the European Parliament; and

- ❖ the function of high representative for foreign and defense policy of the Union should be combined with that of the member of the European Commission in charge of foreign relations.

Enlargement

- ❖ The European Union should ensure that its internal reforms are sufficiently advanced by 2004 that new members can be accepted, as decided at the EU Gothenburg Summit in June 2001.

The enlargement of the European Union is important for the stability of Central and Eastern Europe and ideally should proceed in tandem with the enlargement of NATO. A Union enlarged to twenty-seven or more members will not be able to contribute to that stability, however, if the Union is too weak internally to be effective.

Common Policy Regarding North America

For a healthy transatlantic relationship that contributes to a stable peace in Europe, the European Union needs a clear and consistent policy regarding its relations with North America. It will be a major challenge for the Union to develop a common policy that rises above generalities, but the issues involved are central to strengthening the Union while building a stable peace in Europe. A common policy should deal with security as well as economic issues.

Essential elements:

❖ The European Union should give priority to the formulation of a positive strategy toward North America and the Atlantic Alliance. This strategy should be discussed with the U.S. government.

❖ Europe, which we assume wants a U.S. and Canadian military presence in Europe indefinitely and therefore wishes to cooperate closely with the United States and Canada, should not base its common foreign policy on a premise of opposition to "American hegemony."

❖ The European Union should indicate to its North American allies the conditions under which it is prepared to contribute to peace-keeping and peace-enforcing activities outside Europe, both with and without a mandate from the UN Security Council.

Decisions will be made as circumstances arise, but previous discussion of principles may avoid lengthy disputes in moments of crisis.

❖ The Union's economy must remain open toward its partners.

Rather than trying to become a self-contained economic zone, the Union should continue to support free trade. As noted above, the New Transatlantic Agenda and other transatlantic channels should be used to discuss trade conflicts in the Euroatlantic area at expert levels before minor conflicts threaten to become major.

RUSSIA AND THE WEST

4. We believe that the United States and the members of the European Union should make a greater effort to act consistently in their relations with Russia, notwithstanding the occasional differences of opinion between the two sides of the Atlantic. Their policies should reflect a mutual desire to accept Russia as the "normal" nation it wishes to be, with all that implies for behavior on both sides.

The following principles illustrate the spirit that should motivate the United States and the European Union in their dealings with Russia.

❖ Approach Russia with an open mind and involve it as much as possible in a dialogue regarding the whole of the Euroatlantic area, conflict prevention, and peacekeeping and peace-enforcing operations. Russia should be treated neither as the superpower that it is no longer nor as a *quantité négligeable.* Russian membership in NATO at a future date should be an option.

❖ Remain ready to provide more expertise to Russia when so requested—for example, to help establish a free market economy or to bolster the rule of law—but do not treat Russia as a pupil in need of teaching.

❖ Quietly but consistently tell Russia that no close ties or lasting cooperation can be established, and no major Western investments or loans will be forthcoming, unless Russia respects human rights and observes fundamental principles of democracy, the rule of law, and the free market.

❖ Hold Russian authorities responsible for human rights violations but on each occasion make a careful choice between public protests and quiet diplomacy. Western diplomatic approaches to the Russian government should preferably be made on the basis of obligations to which the Russian government has already subscribed.

5. We recommend that the New Transatlantic Agenda forum should be used to coordinate Western support for Russia in such fields as development of a stable democracy, observance of human rights, and maintenance of the rule of law.

Such support should generally be given in the form of expertise and training—for instance, for politicians in the rules of democracy, for judges and lawyers in the maintenance of the rule of law, for human rights workers in the best ways to defend human rights, and for journalists in the management of an independent and responsible press. While much help in these fields has been offered to the Russians since the fall of the Soviet Union, Western efforts have often been disjointed and without overall coordination. More targeted support should more effectively assist Russia in becoming a stable, democratic, and prosperous partner of the West.

6. We believe that Russia, for its part, should actively strive to find its new international identity in a constructive relationship, rather than in opposition to the United States and the European Union. The key notion is Russia *as a European country* and not *a power in Europe.*

Russia has its own perspective on dealing with the West; its views should be understood in terms of Russian history, Russian culture, and Russian self-identity (that is, the sense of what it is to be a Russian today, at the beginning of twenty-first century, not during the Soviet and imperial periods). Russia expects to be a part of a European security framework and wants its legitimate interests respected and accommodated. Russia also has important and even vital interests in Asia and in the former Soviet south, where much of the Soviet natural wealth was located and where dangerous sources of instability are emerging. The West has a big stake in the final form of the post-Soviet, postimperial "Russian idea," which is now being developed.

From a Russian perspective, the most practical and effective way to demilitarize Russia's relations with the West is through Russia's consistent and increasingly deep integration with the European Union at both multilateral and bilateral levels. The more interdependent and intertwined Russia and the European Union become, the more difficult it will be for anyone to continue to pretend that NATO (largely composed of EU member-states) can be a security threat to Russia.

A part of the process of demilitarizing the relationship is to actively engage those groups within the Russian body politic, as well as within Russia's business and security communities, that continue to regard the West, especially the United States, with suspicion. For the geopolitically conscious circles in Russia, emphasis should be placed on Russian-Western cooperation in managing instability and addressing the new security threats in the greater Middle East. For Russia's defense and defense-related industries, positive change can be effected by engaging in long-term joint ventures with U.S. and/or European firms. For the military, this can be done by undertaking joint peace operations, from the Balkans to Moldova to the Caucasus.

Ultimately, however, it is Russia's own domestic transformation toward a democratic, market-oriented society based on the rule of law and respect for human rights that will underpin a new relationship, a relationship that goes beyond the traditional calculations of military balance and geopolitical competition.

A Targeted Trilateral Agenda[4]

7. We believe that habits of cooperation between the United States, the European Union, and Russia should be fostered through a mix of specific security, political, and economic measures accepted by each of them.

The remainder of this chapter presents sixteen suggestions for short-term initiatives in the following areas: security; trade and the economy; and health, education, environmental protection, and civil society.

Security

i. NATO heads of state and government and the Russian president should hold a formal meeting of the NATO-Russia Permanent Joint Council.

The first objective would be to achieve more results from the PfP. Priority areas for discussion should include

- ❖ creating greater mutual transparency in national defense planning and budgeting processes;
- ❖ enhancing joint planning, training, and exercises, especially for peacekeeping purposes;
- ❖ taking steps to promote the capacity for joint operations; and
- ❖ designating military units for future peacekeeping and antiterrorist activities authorized by the United Nations or the OSCE.

The second objective would be to strengthen the consultative mechanism of the Permanent Joint Council. As a result of the terrorist attacks in September 2001, agreement has already been reached on frequent meetings of experts to discuss antiterrorism measures. Other issues identified in the NATO-Russia Founding Act should be regularly discussed in the same way. Leaders should further agree on an agenda for the Permanent Joint Council that will include sharing the results of research and development activities regarding ballistic missile defense and cooperation in early warning of ballistic missile launches. The NATO-Russia Founding Act should be reviewed with an eye to adapting it to address the varied security challenges of the twenty-first century.

The NATO connection can and should be used to foster a more inclusive security community centered on Europe. Events in the recent past, however, have worked against that possibility. One such event was NATO's role in the Balkans, which caused Russian resentment against the West. Another was Russia's war in Chechnya, which discouraged the West from engaging in military-to-military contacts with Russia. The excessive caution on the part of the Russian military in making full use of the opportunities provided by the PfP and the NATO-Russia Permanent Joint Council stems in large part from a lingering view of NATO as the enemy—a legacy of the Cold War that will take time to disappear.

ii. Russia and the NATO member-states should study the possibility of a joint NATO-Russia project of research, development, production, and deployment of a defense against ballistic missiles.

This project would be directed, in the first instance, at countering threats from areas geographically close to Europe. NATO and Russia could form a partnership to manage a missile defense project that might involve some form of joint production, technology sharing, and cost sharing. Russia's S-300 air defense missile could become part of a European air and missile defense system, together with other U.S.- or European-designed theater missile defense (TMD) systems. Many models for such cooperation exist. Some of them involve multinational teamwork in developing technology for the project.[5]

Should a TMD program for Europe with NATO and Russian participation become a reality, a material foundation of Euroatlantic security would have been constructed for the first time. The United States, the European Union, and Russia could develop joint threat assessment procedures, a joint decision-making mechanism (but probably not for command and control), and a common weapons arsenal. Integration among them would be even closer than currently exists among the NATO Allies.

A joint NATO-Russia program need not supplant more ambitious U.S. plans for a U.S. national missile defense system, nor require immediate abrogation of the 1972 Anti-Ballistic Missile Treaty, which forbids the development of the larger-scale defenses envisioned in most national missile defense proposals.

A Europe-first missile defense policy, in fact, would be an essential building block for any effective U.S. national missile defense program. The technology for joint defense in Europe will be available sooner and more reliably than the more experimental systems required for U.S. national missile defense.

As regards national missile defense, nothing the United States can deploy in the next ten to fifteen years will be able to eliminate the Russian deterrent potential vis-à-vis the United States.[6] Based on experience working together on TMD in Europe, Russia and the United

States should be able to find ways to modify the 1972 Anti-Ballistic Missile Treaty and to limit a U.S. missile defense system so as to meet both countries' security concerns and preserve strategic stability.

iii. A joint review should be conducted by as many nations of the Euroatlantic community as care to participate of current and prospective export controls for defense materials, software, and technology that could be used for the development and production of weapons of mass destruction. In addition, international cooperation in combating terrorism should be added to the agenda of regular discussions between the European Union, Russia, and the United States, and a special subgroup of the NATO-Russia Permanent Joint Council should be established to address this issue.

Several international treaties and agreements link the nations of this region together in the fight against the spread of weapons of mass destruction (nuclear, biological, and chemical). These include the Nuclear Nonproliferation Treaty, the biological and chemical weapons conventions, and other, more informal, regimes such as the Missile Technology Control Regime (MTCR) that reinforce these formal treaties. It has been difficult to agree on rules concerning exports, especially of dual-use technology and equipment. Cooperation in intelligence and law enforcement is needed both to fight terrorism and to track and prevent illicit traffic in arms.[7]

Terrorism and the proliferation of weapons of mass destruction and of their means of delivery (ballistic and cruise missiles, for example) are threats to Russia, the members of the European Union, and the United States. The threats are not limited to them—they are truly a global problem. The members of an incipient European security community, because of the assets they control, have an unparalleled ability to do something about these threats.

iv. Major arms suppliers should consider market-sharing arrangements.

One possibility would be to recognize a Russian share in markets where Russian-built arms have formed the bulk of national inventories and where these arms can still be modernized and upgraded. Consideration also should be given to cooperating with Russian arms suppliers in codevelopment and coproduction of weapons systems (for example, aircraft). This is a difficult task, but politically and strategically it is sure to pay great dividends.

Russian arms sales, in particular to Iran but also to China and India, are seen in the West, and in the United States especially, as a major factor contributing to the deterioration of U.S.-Russian relations. Critics should consider a few points before reaching judgments. First, Russia's entire defense budget in FY 2001 was only $7.5 billion. It is perhaps understandable that Russian arms exports, which average $3 billion per year, are critical to the survival of the Russian defense industrial base. Second, stiff and, in Russian eyes, unfair competition from U.S. arms manufacturers has virtually cut off the Russians from the lucrative markets of pro-Western states in the Persian Gulf, Central Europe, Eastern Europe, and elsewhere and has consigned the Russians to dealing with the "ghetto" of customers to whom the West will not sell arms. Third, distrust between Russia and the United States prevents serious discussion of issues pertaining to arms and technology exports. The United States suspects Russia of cheating on its international commitments relating to the Missile Technology Control Regime, while Russia believes that the United States is practicing double standards aimed at shutting Russia out of the last remaining arms markets.

v. The European Union countries should jointly increase their financial and technical support for the protection of weapons-usable fissile materials stored in Russia. The United States, which has been providing financial and technical support for several years under the Nunn-Lugar legislation, should continue this program and raise its funding levels by at least 50 percent.[8]

Disposing of the nuclear legacy of the Cold War is an urgent task for all members of a nascent security community centered on Europe.

Environmental problems traceable to nuclear arms built during the Cold War have been identified both in Russia and in the United States. Difficulties in protecting and accounting for fissile materials have arisen in Russia and elsewhere. Thefts of fissile material already have occurred. The resources devoted to dealing with these problems have not been on a scale comparable to the size of the disasters that stray or stolen fissile materials can cause, not to mention the damage that already has been done to the environment. Economic dislocations in Russia have affected its ability to deal with this Cold War legacy.

vi. The nations of the European Union, Russia, and the United States, with a view to encouraging cooperation among themselves, should find a suitable means of discussing issues created by regional conflicts.

Such discussion could be pursued in the NATO-Russia Permanent Joint Council, the PfP framework, or the OSCE. Possibilities for cooperation exist with respect to Southeastern Europe, Central Asia, and the Persian Gulf. In addition to economic assistance to countries in those areas, military-to-military activities between Russia and the NATO member-states on subjects such as the development of common norms and procedures for peacekeeping and peace enforcement could be very valuable.

vii. The European Union, Russia, and the United States should launch a dialogue on the use of military force in connection with humanitarian interventions.

This dialogue should seek to develop a consensus on rules concerning conditions and circumstances that would justify military interventions. Otherwise, continuing disagreements on the fundamentals of the issue will generate serious tensions among the three parties. "Track-two diplomacy"—that is, contacts among nongovernmental specialists with knowledge of their governments' attitudes and policies— may be the best way to proceed.

Trade and the Economy

viii. Russia, the European Union, and the United States should adopt as an objective Russian membership in the WTO no later than 2005; they should also discuss on an annual basis and in appropriate EU-Russian-U.S. and EU-Russian forums barriers to Russian exports within the region.

Russia applied for membership in the WTO in 1995, has made the required offer of conditions governing access to the Russian market to the WTO, and is holding bilateral talks with WTO members. President Bush has stated that he believes "Russia ought to be admitted into the World Trade Organization—and we'll work toward that end."[9] Russia's goal is entry in 2002. That is probably an optimistic timetable, but the issue of Russian membership should not be allowed to drag on without resolution. Of course, Russia's own willingness to cut tariffs is crucial to the success of its application.

Foreign trade is important for economic progress throughout the region. However, unless the issue is managed skillfully, trade can be highly divisive. Russian exports are mainly in the form of raw materials —oil and gas, in particular—and need to be diversified. Direct foreign investment would help to accomplish this goal. Barriers against Russian exports in the form of tariffs, nontariff barriers, and antidumping legislation need to be removed to the extent that fair trade permits.

ix. The World Bank should assume a larger role in working with Russians at the local and regional levels on infrastructure development, including public health. The United States and the European Union should also make additional funds available for this purpose in their bilateral programs with Russia.

The experience of monetary and financial cooperation between Russia and international financial institutions since 1991 has not been a happy one. Many experts now doubt the wisdom of the advice offered to Russia in the early 1990s. Right or wrong, Moscow did not always take the advice, in any case. And even when Moscow did accept the external recommendations, it could not implement them because of weaknesses in Russia's central government mechanisms, including those for raising taxes and economic restructuring.

Russia's infrastructure needs are immense in all parts of the country. Cooperation in fixing problems at the grassroots level will improve morale, direct scarce development funds to places where they are needed, and encourage local governments and local entrepreneurs to make the investments needed to build the foundations for a healthy economy.

x. Continuing attention must be given to the restructuring of Russia's foreign debts. Russian actions to encourage reform of the Russian economy should be a consideration affecting debt relief.

The Soviet Union tripled its foreign debt during the Gorbachev era. Eager to get access to the Soviet market for their companies and also to prop up the Gorbachev regime, Western governments gladly extended loans, ignoring the risks. Having assumed debts incurred by the Soviet Union, Russia owes the Paris Club (a group of Western governments) well over $40 billion. Germany holds nearly half of this. Somewhere between $15 billion and $19 billion in interest and principal must be paid by Russia in 2003. This will be difficult for the Russian government to do. Russian finance minister Aleksei Kudrin has been quoted as saying that he hopes Western creditors will agree to restructure the debt with a partial write-off. In May 2000, Deputy Finance Minister Sergei Kolotukhin called for debt forgiveness of "more than 50 percent." There is a precedent: in the fall of 2000, foreign commercial banks in the London Club reduced interest and principal on the debt Russia owed these banks.[10]

Russia's foreign debt is a drag on the nation's economic recovery. Restructuring the debt is a relatively low-cost way of assisting the Russian economy, although it should be done with an eye to what Russia can do to adapt itself to the requirements of the global economy. Various suggestions for a quid pro quo have been floated in the media and in academic literature. One is to trade debt for equity in Russian companies. Reportedly, in January 2001 German chancellor Schroeder and Russian president Putin discussed this idea inconclusively. Of course, Russia was in the midst of an economic boom at that time and Germany holds much of the Russian debt. Other ideas include reforms in the Russian economy. In his joint press conference with Putin on June 16, 2001, Bush mentioned "the rule of law, a reasonable tax system, transparency in the economy" as important considerations for U.S. business. Some specific trade-offs within these rubrics might be reviewed.

xi. The NATO-Russia Permanent Joint Council should establish a forum of experts to develop guidelines for energy cooperation.

Energy is an area where cooperation throughout the region would have beneficial political and economic results. In view of the priority given by the Bush administration to energy policy, this would be a particularly apt subject for Euroatlantic cooperation—indeed, it was discussed by Bush and Putin at their June 2001 meeting. Given the stakes involved and the differences in national interests, individual governments will be hard-pressed to escape from competitive relationships with other governments on energy policy, but mutual economic and commercial advantages should be possible through cooperation. Sharing technologies in fuel efficiency and conservation is another possibility.

xii. Multiple pipelines from the Caspian basin would be the best way of ensuring the security of energy supplies and of promoting energy cooperation between Russia and the West.

The Caspian basin is unlikely to become an area of intense Russian-Western confrontation if heavy-handed moves by either side are avoided. Russia would be well advised to respect the sovereignty of the newly independent states and abstain from crude pressure tactics when dealing with them. Such instruments as military intervention and coups d'état should never be used. A Russian monopoly on oil flows from the Caspian is not viewed kindly by the West but, by the same token, the exclusion of Russia from the Caspian oil business would deeply offend Russia. Thus, multiple pipelines from the basin and joint participation in these operations are essential from the points of view of both the oil industry and the respective governments.

Support for Health, Education, Environmental Protection, and Civil Society

xiii. We recommend a greatly expanded effort to support Russia's health care needs. Support, generally in the form of medical expertise, should be provided directly to local and regional health care centers wherever possible.

Russia's true security problems today are mainly of domestic origin. The demographic situation is especially worrisome. Not only is the population decreasing; it also suffers from high mortality (male life expectancy is only fifty-nine years) caused by alcoholism and drug addiction as well as by disease. An AIDS epidemic is looming. In a globalizing world, Russia's health problems may affect not only its immediate neighbors but also other countries in Europe as well as the United States. Helping the Russians improve their health care is one of the best ways to enhance the security of the West while at the same time contributing to friendlier relations with Russia.[11]

Medical expertise, medicines, and medical equipment, when these cannot be produced in Russia itself, should be provided directly on a scale sufficient to alleviate the severe shortages that exist in Russia. Programs to encourage exchanges of information regarding clinical techniques should be an important part of this effort. Funds for this purpose could be derived from a consortium of U.S. and EU economic assistance agencies, and perhaps augmented by the World Bank. Expert advice should be sought from private and public medical organizations to define the parameters of the program.

Since the Russian Ministry of Health has rejected World Bank assistance in combating AIDS and tuberculosis, direct support for local Russian medical centers should be emphasized.

xiv. An expanded joint effort should be made under the auspices of the World Bank to improve environmental conditions in Russia and elsewhere in Eastern Europe.

The almost total disregard by the communist command economy of the environmental consequences of its decisions has caused disastrous pollution in Russia and other states of the former communist bloc. This pollution, which also threatens other parts of Europe, can be dealt with only if massive and well-coordinated Western assistance is made available. The categories of pollution requiring cleanup or isolation should be identified and prioritized, and a multiyear fund should be established to support efforts of Russian and Eastern European governments. Wherever practicable these efforts should be linked to economic programs, such as defense conversion.

xv. A tripartite trust fund should be established by Russia, the European Union, and the United States and Canada to make scholarships available to qualified university students who wish to study for a minimum of one academic year in a university outside their own nation (outside the European Union for citizens of EU nations) but within the community defined by North America, the European Union, and Russia.

Generational change could work either for or against a stable peace in a Europe-centered security community. If the generations that come to power in the early years of the twenty-first century display nationalistic, xenophobic, unilateralist, or isolationist tendencies, then the best that the Euroatlantic area can expect will be the perpetuation of a conditional peace. However, if young people learn to live comfortably within an extended Europe that is peaceful, undivided, and democratic, and if they find opportunities in globalization "with a human face," then they will strongly support the development of a stable peace. The number of university students from the United States, Russia, and the European Union currently studying in one another's universities is strikingly low. Boosting this number could encourage the emergence of a more favorable attitude toward cooperation in building a stable peace.[12]

xvi. Private institutions in the United States and within the European Union should significantly increase their support for nongovernmental organizations (NGOs) in Russia.

President Putin has written of the cardinal importance to Russia's democratic future of a civil society. In his 2000 New Year's statement, he expressed the need to "create conditions to foster the creation of a civil society that will be a counterweight and control on the executive."[13] NGOs could become as important in Russia as they are in the United States and in EU countries in offering "counterweights" to official stances. Russian NGOs have found it difficult to establish themselves, partly for financial reasons and partly because there is no strong tradition of private citizens' organizations in Russia. Indeed, any external support for Russian NGOs must be extended with great care and sensitivity.[14] Those organizations that promote the rule of law should be especially encouraged.

CONCLUDING REMARKS

Our proposals offer a coherent program for reconciliation and forward-looking cooperation. We fully realize that some of our ideas may be difficult for our governments and our peoples to accept. Even if they are disposed to cooperate, our nations have a distance to travel before a stable peace will be within reach. Attitudes cannot be expected to change overnight.

The recommendations in this book should be seen as *building blocks*. Each of them is realistic and realizable and will yield solid benefits for all the nations of the Euroatlantic region; none of them demands an irrevocable commitment to take additional steps. They can be put into practice at different times, together or separately. Because we believe that the alternative to embracing a strategy for stable peace will be aimless drift, growing indifference, or even hostility within the extended European system, we urge that the first steps toward a stable peace be taken in the very near future.

Notes

Introduction

1. Speech in Warsaw, Poland, June 15, 2001; text in *New York Times*, June 16, 2001, A6.

2. Alexander George of Stanford University has written about these three types of peace: stable, conditional, and precarious. His work expands upon earlier studies by Kenneth Boulding of the University of Michigan. We have used the definitions George presented in his foreword to J. E. Goodby, *Europe Undivided* (Washington, D.C.: United States Institute of Peace Press, 1998) and in an unpublished paper presented to a Yale University conference on grand strategy convened by Paul Kennedy and John Lewis Gaddis, November 13–15, 1998. George's typology also appears in his foreword to Arie M. Kacowicz, Yaacov Bar-Siman-Tov, Ole Elgstrom, and Magnus Jerneck, eds., *Stable Peace among Nations* (Lanham, Md.: Rowman and Littlefield, 2000). This book is an excellent exploration of stable peace, from both the theoretical and case study points of view. However, our views do not always coincide with opinions expressed in *Stable Peace among Nations*. In particular, we think of stable peace as a condition heavily dependent on similar value systems, a condition not necessarily present in a security community. Thus, we believe that a stable peace takes longer to develop than does a security community.

3. Karl Deutsch and his colleagues also concluded that "military alliances seemed to be relatively poor pathways . . . toward pluralistic integration. . . . To be effective, they had to be associated with nonmilitary steps." Karl W. Deutsch et al., *Political Community and the North Atlantic Area: International Organization in the Light of Historical Experience* (Princeton, N.J.: Princeton University Press, 1957), 202.

In fact, the term "security community" is something of a misnomer, since security issues will have moved into the background among members of the community. Emanuel Adler and Michael Barnett have added new dimensions to the security community idea by examining (1) phases in the development of a security community, (2) a set of indicators sensitive to these phases, and (3) disintegration of security communities. They believe that a "compatibility of core values and a collective identity are necessary for the development of security communities." Emanuel Adler and Michael Barnett, *Security Communities* (Cambridge: Cambridge University Press, 1998), 58.

4. Speech in Warsaw, June 15, 2001.

5. Alexander George has described this as a "Lewis and Clark" approach, where the objective is clear and the means are generally understood but the route is relatively uncertain.

1. The Outlook for a Stable Peace

1. See Edward D. Mansfield and Jack Snyder, "Democratization and War," *Foreign Affairs* 74, no. 3 (May-June 1995): 79–97; and Fareed Zakaria, "The Rise of Illiberal Democracy," *Foreign Affairs* 76, no. 6 (November-December 1997): 22–43.

2. An issue that arises within a community that champions particular values is whether, even though democratic in form, governments are seen as legitimate wielders of power by their partners. The situation in Austria in the winter of 1999–2000 was a case in point: the European Union concluded, in an unprecedented decision, that Austria's ruling coalition should be sanctioned because one of its parties was antidemocratic. The Union, which held itself up as a community of values, reserved to itself the right to censure departures from its norms.

3. The term "subrationally unthinkable" is used by John Mueller in his *Retreat from Doomsday* (New York: Basic Books, 1989). Mueller explains the term as follows:

> War is an idea, and for one to occur a two-step process must be negotiated: first, someone must think of war as a genuine option, and second, when evaluated the war option has to be discovered to be an option worth pursuing. . . . An idea becomes impossible not when it becomes reprehensible or has been renounced, but when it fails to percolate into one's consciousness as a conceivable option. . . . [P]eace is most secure when it gravitates away from conscious rationality to become a subrational, unexamined mental habit.
>
> At first war becomes rationally unthinkable—rejected because it's calculated to be ineffective and/or undesirable. Then it becomes subrationally unthinkable—rejected not because it's a bad idea but because it remains subconscious and never comes up as a coherent possibility. (p. 240)

4. U.S. secretary of state Madeleine Albright, statement before the Senate Foreign Relations Committee, Washington, D.C., October 7, 1997, released by the Office of the Spokesman, U.S. Department of State.

5. Speech in Warsaw, Poland, June 15, 2001, as reported in the *New York Times,* June 16, 2001, A6.

6. Press conference of President Bill Clinton, Madrid, Spain, July 9, 1997; press release from the Office of the Press Secretary, the White House.

7. Several years ago Harvard professor Stanley Hoffmann wrote about the shift from a world dominated by the strategic-diplomatic chessboard to a world divided into a variety of chessboards. Hoffmann also pointed to the need for a synthesis in foreign policy between the hard realities of power politics and the demands of the other chessboards.

8. This idea is generally ascribed to Immanuel Kant's 1795 essay "Perpetual Peace." Naturally, scholars continue to debate its truth and relevance. For an excellent discussion of the pros and cons, see M. E. Brown, S. M. Lynn-Jones, and S. E. Miller, eds., *Debating the Democratic Peace* (Cambridge, Mass.: MIT Press, 1996). A more recent, and positive, assessment of democratic peace may be found in Bruce Russett and John Oneal, *Triangulating Peace* (New York: W. W. Norton, 2001).

9. Based on data in Steven Kull (principal investigator), *Seeking a New Balance* (College Park, Md.: Program on International Policy Attitudes, School of Public Affairs, University of Maryland, June 1998).

10. For more on this topic from a U.S. perspective, see Steven Kull and I. M. Destler, *Misreading the Public* (Washington, D.C.: Brookings Institution, 1999), esp. 230–231; and James M. Lindsay, "The New Apathy," *Foreign Affairs* 79, no. 5 (September-October 2000): 2–8.

11. See chapter 2 for a fuller discussion of the issue. Many Western and some Russian observers of current developments in Russia have noted the drag imposed by authoritarian traditions, but Yegor Gaidar, a reformist former prime minister of Russia, may be right that the Russian people, as in postrevolutionary situations elsewhere, are looking for leaders who can restore law and order while maintaining the political achievements of the revolution.

12. Text of the joint press conference by President Bush and President Putin on June 16, 2001, made available by the Office of the Press Secretary, the White House.

13. See Adler and Barnett, *Security Communities,* for a discussion of the rise and decline of security communities.

14. See Zakaria, "Rise of Illiberal Democracy," for a discussion of "constitutional liberalism," or the development of democratic means of governance as a necessary element in democratization.

15. President George W. Bush alluded to this potential for action on a global scale in his Warsaw speech of June 15, 2001: "our trans-Atlantic community must have priorities beyond the consolidation of European peace."

2. The Russian Angle

1. This realization was evident in Vladimir Putin's first major article published on the Internet at the end of 1999 (see *Nezavisimaya Gazeta*, December 30, 1999) and in his first state of the nation address to the Russian parliament as president (July 8, 2000).

2. This was a forum that grew out of the 1996 Shanghai agreement, which finalized the border between the former Soviet republics and China. The parties to the agreement included China, Russia, Kazakhstan, Kyrgyzstan, and Tajikistan. At the 2000 summit, Uzbekistan was present as an observer. There are indications that other Asian countries may consider joining in. In June 2001, the forum became the Shanghai Cooperation Organization upon signature of a new charter by the leaders of the five states.

3. Take, for example, the cover story in the Christmas 1999 issue of the *Economist*: "A Bleak and Bloody Russia."

4. See chapter 4 for a contrasting American perspective on U.S. public opinion.

5. This was signed in May 1992 in Tashkent. Since 1999 its membership has shrunk to Armenia, Belarus, Kazakhstan, Kyrgyzstan, Russia, and Tajikistan.

6. Its milestones included Mikhail Gorbachev's historic trip to China in 1989; the border agreements of 1991 and 1994; the demilitarization and confidence-building agreements of 1996; the declaration on strategic partnership of 1996; and the launching of the Shanghai process in 1996.

7. In his July 2000 state of the nation address, President Putin quoted demographic statistics that indicated that Russia's population was declining at the annual rate of 750,000. The forecast Putin cited warned that by 2015 the Russian population would have decreased by twenty-two million, or one-seventh. This forecast is clearly one of the more pessimistic and does not account for immigration into Russia from other former Soviet states. Still, the general trend is unmistakable.

8. See, for example, President Putin's June 2000 proposal to create a TMD system for Europe with Russian, European, and American participation.

9. See, for example, the Russian public's genuine support for the second Chechen war.

3. Western European Attitudes

1. See "The Council of the European Union and the Common Foreign and Security Policy" (undated), issued by the press service of the Council of the European Union, www.consilium.eu.int/pesc/default.asp?lang=en.

2. For the text of the "Presidential Conclusions" of the Gothenburg summit, see the Web site of the European Council, www.ue.eu.int/newsroom/main.cfm?LANG=1.

3. The document can be found on the EU Web site: www.europa.eu.int.

4. These tasks, elaborated during a conference of the Western European Union in the "Petersberg" conference center near Bonn, include peace-enforcing, peacekeeping, humanitarian, and crisis management operations. See www.weu.int/eng/documents.html.

5. Putin made this statement after a summit meeting with the EU leaders in Paris in October 2000. See *International Herald Tribune,* October 31, 2000, 6.

6. There is, however, more opposition inside Russia to the Union's inclusion of the Baltic states than to that of other prospective members.

7. See the declaration of Robert Schuman, drafted by Jean Monnet, at www.france.diplomatie.fr/archives/europe/module03_4.html.

8. The full text can be found on the Web site of the German Foreign Office: www.auswaertiges-amt.government.de.

9. The word "dreaming" was used by the French interior minister, Jean-Pierre Chëvènement, in a television interview. See *International Herald Tribune,* May 22, 2000, 7.

10. Full text at www.spd.de.

11. Full text at www.elysee.fr.

12. This expression was used by Pierre Moscovici, French deputy-minister in charge of European affairs; see www.finance.diplomatie.fr/avenir.

13. Full text at www.france.diplomatie.fr/avenir/jospin280501.gb.html.

14. The full text can be found at www.number-10.gov.uk.

15. For details, see the NATO Web site, www.nato.int, or the *NATO Handbook* issued by the Bureau of Information and Press of NATO in Brussels.

16. The full text can be found at www.pub.whitehouse.gov.

17. *International Herald Tribune,* May 29, 2000, 9.

18. For documentation, see www.osce.org.

19. See the WEU Web site: www.weu.int.

20. *International Herald Tribune,* April 18, 2000, op-ed page.

21. *Economist,* May 13, 2001, 14.

Another View from Europe

1. Hubert Védrine et Dominique Moïsi, *Les Cartes de la France à l'heure de la Mondialisation* (Paris: Librarie Fayart, 2000).

2. The Cologne (June 1999) and Helsinki (December 1999) meetings of the European Council (heads of state and government) defined the defense goals of the Union.

3. The council, for general affairs, normally meets at the level of foreign ministers.

4. See note 4, chapter 3.

5. The first conference for Euro-Mediterranean partnership was held in Barcelona in 1995. Its purpose was to create an area of peace, development, and mutual understanding between the fifteen members of the European Union and the twelve countries of the southern Mediterranean (Algeria, Cyprus, Egypt, Israel, Jordan, Lebanon, Malta, Morocco, the Palestinian Authority, Syria, Tunisia, and Turkey). This process has been maintained but has suffered from the consequences of the Israeli-Palestinian conflict. The fourth meeting, held in Marseilles in November 2000, was not attended by either Syria or Lebanon.

6. The Lomé agreements have, since 1963, promoted political and economic cooperation between the members of the European Union and a group of countries that were all African originally but that now include some states of the Caribbean and Pacific areas. The most recent convention, signed in Cotonou, Benin, in June 2000, covers the prevention of conflicts and support for democracy as well as aid for development and trade.

4. An American Perspective

1. Speech of February 26, 1999, San Francisco; text made available by the Office of the Press Secretary, the White House.

2. Ibid.

3. The full text can be found at www.pub.whitehouse.gov.

4. Remarks by the president to students and faculty of the National Defense University; press release by the Office of the Press Secretary, the White House, May 1, 2001.

5. Speech in Warsaw, June 15, 2001, as reported in the *New York Times,* June 16, 2001, A6.

6. Joint press conference of President Bush and President Putin in Slovenia, June 16, 2001; text made available by the Office of the Press Secretary, the White House.

7. Secretary Powell used the phrase "we went in together and we'll come out together" repeatedly in comments to the press to signify cohesion in the Balkans. President Bush, in his Warsaw speech of June 15, 2001, said "we went into the Balkans together and we will come out together"; *New York Times,* June 16, 2001, A6.

8. In a 1998 U.S. Information Agency poll, asked whether political unification of Europe is mostly a good thing or mostly a bad thing for their country, 58 percent of Americans saw European unification as a good thing for the United States, 59 percent of the Germans saw it as good for Germany, 34 percent of the British saw it as good for Britain, and 54 percent of the French saw it as good for France. Kull, *Seeking a New Balance,* 23. In a poll conducted during 1998 by the Program on International Policy Attitudes, 72.2 percent of the Americans polled agreed that the United States and the European Union "should be more willing to make decisions jointly, even if this means that the U.S. as well as Europe will sometimes have to go along with a policy that is not its first choice." Kull, *Seeking a New Balance,* 79.

9. One such view of U.S.-European relations was expressed in the pages of the *New York Times* following Denmark's referendum rejecting the euro:

> [T]he Clinton administration has always said European unification is in America's interest, and formally supported the euro, [but] the strategic attraction to Washington of a federal United States of Europe has never been entirely clear.
>
> But a democratic Europe at peace, cooperating economically without integrating politically, heterogeneous rather than monolithic, poses no such problems. For it offers the United States a vast and stable market, without the European political cohesion that might one day counter or offset American strategic dominance.

Roger Cohen, "More a Loop Than a Knot," *New York Times,* September 30, 2000, 1.

10. Kull, *Seeking a New Balance,* 20.

11. Zbigniew Brzezinski, "A Geostrategy for Eurasia," *Foreign Affairs* 76, no. 5 (September-October 1997): 53.

12. Stephen M. Walt, "The Precarious Partnership: America and Europe," in *Atlantic Security: Contending Visions,* ed. Charles A. Kupchan (New York: Council on Foreign Relations, 1998), 35.

13. The *New York Times'* Western Europe correspondent, Roger Cohen, quoted the German defense minister, Rudolph Scharping, as follows: "As the European Union develops its security and defense policy and becomes an independent actor, we must determine our security policy with Russia, our biggest neighbor." Cohen said the idea "is chilling for the United States." *New York Times,* February 11, 2001, 4.

14. An example is Michael McFaul's article in the *Washington Post,* June 9, 2001, A18: "He [Putin] consistently states that Russia must become more integrated with European institutions, but at the same time he undertakes antidemocratic policies at home that make it more difficult for Russia to join these Western clubs."

15. See, for example, Michael McFaul and Sarah E. Mendelson, "Russian Democracy—A U.S. National Security Interest," *Demokratizatsiya* 8, no. 3 (summer 2000): 330–353; and Celeste Wallander, *The Multiple Dimensions of Russian Threat Assessment,* Policy Memo Series no. 199 (Washington, D.C.: Program on New Approaches to Russian Security, Council on Foreign Relations, April 2001).

16. Timothy J. Colton and Michael McFaul, *Are Russians Undemocratic?* Working Paper no. 20 (Washington, D.C.: Russian and Eurasian Program, Carnegie Endowment for International Peace, June 2000). Polling was done in 1999 and 2000.

17. Astrid S. Tuminez, *Western Perceptions of Russian Nationalism,* Policy Memo Series no. 193 (Washington, D.C.: Program on New Approaches to Russian Security, Council on Foreign Relations, March 2001).

18. For a vivid description of the problems Russia faced in 1999, see David Hoffman, "A State of Lawlessness," *Washington Post,* September 9, 1999, A1. Reforms being pushed by Putin in 2001 are summarized in Peter Baker and Susan B. Glasser, "Putin Pushes Reforms, with Power," *Washington Post,* July 7, 2001, A1.

19. For a discussion of this by one practitioner, see James Goodby, "Reflections on Russian Government Policymaking," in *The Nuclear Turning Point,* ed. H. A. Feiveson (Washington, D.C.: Brookings Institution Press, 1999), 189–190. According to Goodby, "Yeltsin seemed unable to prevent his government from reversing earlier presidential decisions or ignoring them."

20. Joint press conference of President Bush and President Putin in Slovenia, June 16, 2001.

21. Kull, *Seeking a New Balance,* 85.

22. Poll taken in March 2000 by the Gallup Organization. Published by the Gallup Poll, March 22, 2000. This and the following poll data are available online from the Roper Center for Public Opinion Research, University of Connecticut, at www.ropercenter.uconn.edu/ipoll; and from the Web site of the Program on International Policy Attitudes (PIPA), University of Maryland, www.americans-world.org.

23. Poll taken in May 2000 by the Princeton Survey Research Associates. Published in *The People and the Press Political Survey,* May 11, 2000.

24. Poll taken in September 1999 by the Hart and Teeter Research Companies. Published by NBC/Wall Street Journal Poll, September 1999.

25. Poll taken in July 1999 by the Hart and Teeter Research Companies. Published by NBC News/Wall Street Journal Poll, August 1999.

26. Poll taken in May 2000 by the Gallup Organization. Published by the Gallup Poll on May 24, 2000.

27. Poll taken in March 1999 by Princeton Survey Research Associates. Published by the News Interest Index Poll on April 8, 1999.

28. Poll taken in March 1999 by the *Los Angeles Times.* Published by the Los Angeles Times Poll on March 26, 1999.

29. These polling data from the Gallup Poll were provided by PIPA.

30. Zbigniew Brzezinski has written on this point in "Strategic Dialogue in St. Petersburg," *Washington Post*, January 5, 2001, A21. His conclusion: "Russia's only hopeful future is, indeed, in Europe. But it is in a Europe that is truly democratic and that knows its global role involves an organic connection with America. And only accommodation to such a Europe will permit Russia to become a modern, democratic, prosperous and thus influential member of the growing Euro-Atlantic community." See also Rene Nyberg, "The Baltic as an Interface between the EU and Russia" (paper presented at the Sixth World Congress of the International Council for Central and East European Studies, Tampere, Finland, June 29, 2000). A leading Finnish observer of the Russian scene, Nyberg has supported the notion that Russia should strive to fulfill the Maastricht and Copenhagen criteria so as to be in a position to integrate with European structures, even though Russia is not a member of the European Union.

31. For further discussion of Russia's evolving foreign policy, see Deborah Larson and Alexei Shevchenko, "Bringing Russia into the Club," in *Preventing Deadly Conflict among Nations: Creating a New Encompassing Coalition,* ed. Richard Rosecrance (Lanham, Md.: Rowman and Littlefield, forthcoming). See also U.S. and Russian Working Groups, *U.S.-Russian Relations at the Turn of the Century* (Washington, D.C.: Carnegie Endowment for International Peace; Moscow: Council on Foreign and Defense Policy, 2000).

32. Henry A. Kissinger, *Diplomacy* (New York: Simon and Schuster, 1994), 55.

33. A scholarly criticism of the Senate's 1999 vote on the test ban treaty was Joseph Nye's view that it amounted to squandering U.S. "soft power": the ability to attract rather than coerce. Joseph S. Nye, "The Power We Must Not Squander," *New York Times,* January 3, 2000, A23.

34. Thomas Friedman has argued that "we can't manage such an integrated system [the global economy] alone, and if we try we will stimulate a coalition against us" (*New York Times,* October 27, 1999, A31). Jim Hoagland has written that "U.S. policymakers and legislators are missing the wider repercussions of their deeds and words on cooperative international efforts to limit the spread—and importance —of nuclear weapons as the 21st century begins. . . . Congress and the White House must not let unilateralism be the only option available to Americans" (*Washington Post,* October 31, 1999, B7).

35. Another American scholar, Charles Kupchan, is probably right when he argues that even though strategic restraint is becoming an embedded feature of international politics there remains a need for structural sources of stability. He means by this a relationship among the important nations that is influenced by an international regime that generates predictability and order. See Charles Kupchan, "After Pax Americana," *International Security* 23, no. 2 (fall 1998): 40–79.

36. Quoted by William Drozdiak, "We Simply Disagree," *Washington Post,* June 17, 2001, A1.

37. Robert Kagan and William Kristol, "Europe Whole and Free," *Washington Post,* October 8, 2000, B7.

38. Robert Kagan, "A Good Week's Work . . . ," *Washington Post,* June 18, 2001, A17.

39. Anthony Lake, "Our Place in the Balkans," *New York Times,* October 8, 2000.

40. Essentially the same point was made by Condoleeza Rice in "Promoting the National Interest," *Foreign Affairs* 79, no. 1 (January-February 2000): 49: "This polarized view—you are either a realist or devoted to norms and values—may be just fine in academic debate, but it is a disaster for American foreign policy."

41. See Kupchan, "After Pax Americana."

42. See J. E. Goodby, "The Context of Korean Unification: The Case for a Multilateral Security Structure," in *Security in Korea,* ed. P. Williams, D. M. Goldstein, and H. L. Andrews (Boulder, Colo.: Westview, 1994).

5. Policies for a Stable Peace

1. These data are taken from Keith Bush, *The Russian Economy in February 2001* (Washington, D.C.: Center for Strategic and International Studies, 2001).

2. Results of a poll conducted in 1998, referred to in Yury Levada, "Ot mnenii k ponimaniyu," in *Sociologicheskie ocherki, 1993–2000* (Moscow: Moscow School of Political Studies, 2000), 358.

3. President Putin remarked during the course of his joint press conference with President Bush on June 16, 2001, that "the differences in our positions . . . really are not of a fundamental nature, a global nature, something which cannot be solved —not at all." Text of the joint press conference made available by the Office of the Press Secretary, the White House. In his Warsaw speech on June 15, 2001, speaking of Europe and the United States, Bush said, "our goals are large, and our differences, in comparison, are small." See *New York Times*, June 16, 2001, A6.

4. A debate has been under way in the West for some time regarding the wisdom of economic policies that governments and the International Monetary Fund recommended to Yeltsin's government. An analysis from the point of view that it was wrong to insist on transferring Western economic concepts to a Russia that was far from ready for this can be found in Peter Reddaway and Dmitri Glinski, *The Tragedy of Russia's Reforms: Market Bolshevism against Democracy* (Washington, D.C.: United States Institute of Peace Press, 2001).

5. This section draws, in part, on ideas contained in chapter 8 of Goodby, *Europe Undivided.*

6. *International Herald Tribune*, October 31, 2000, 6.

7. This section draws on discussions at a conference sponsored by the United States Institute of Peace, "Defining Russia's Role," at the Royal Institute of International Affairs in London (Chatham House), October 11–13, 2000.

8. These goals were defined in J. E. Goodby, "Introductory Remarks," in *Regional Conflicts: The Challenge to U.S.-Russian Cooperation,* ed. J. E. Goodby (Oxford: SIPRI and Oxford University Press, 1995), 3–4.

9. NATO's war with Yugoslavia had a major impact on Ukrainian public opinion, according to polling data. In October 2000, the Kiev International Institute of Sociology conducted a poll that indicated that 52 percent of those polled thought Ukraine should seek closer security relations with Russia and the Commonwealth of Independent States, while only 14 percent favored the United States and NATO. Cited in Mark Kramer, *Ukraine, Russia, and U.S. Policy,* Policy Memo Series no. 191 (Washington, D.C.: Program on New Approaches to Russian Security, Council on Foreign Relations, April 2001).

10. In an interview with American correspondents in Moscow on June 18, 2001, President Putin said that it was "not a fundamental question to us whether Chechnya becomes independent or stays within Russia." Patrick E. Tyler, "Putin Says Russia Would Add Arms to Counter Shield," *New York Times,* June 19, 2001, A1.

11. Putin remarked at the Bush-Putin press conference on June 16, 2001, that the two leaders had talked about the Caspian basin and said that "very soon the new pipeline system is going to go into effect, which is going to be transporting energy resources from the Caspian region through Novie Russkie [referring to the Caspian Pipeline Consortium from Tengiz to Novorossisk]. And this is a joint project of two companies—Russian and American companies. I'm sure that this will not be the last such project." Text provided by the White House. The Bush administration has invited Russian companies to join in an alternate pipeline through Azerbaijan, Georgia, and Turkey—the Baku-Tbilisi-Ceyhan (BTC) route. For a useful discussion of these issues, see Douglas W. Blum, *America's Caspian Policy under the Bush Administration,* Policy Memo Series no. 190 (Washington, D.C.: Program on New Approaches to Russian Security, Council on Foreign Relations, March 2001).

12. Putin spoke with foreign journalists in Moscow on June 18, 2001, about his meeting with Bush on June 16, 2001. Tyler, "Putin Says Russia Would Add Arms to Counter Shield."

13. See also note 2, chapter 2. For a typical U.S. assessment of implications for the United States, see Patrick E. Tyler, "Bush and Putin Look Each Other in the Eye," *New York Times,* June 17, 2001, A8.

14. As reported by Reuters; see *International Herald Tribune,* October 31, 2000.

15. P. Terrence Hopmann, "The OSCE: Its Contribution to Conflict Prevention and Resolution," in *International Conflict Resolution after the Cold War,* ed. P. C. Stern and D. Druckman (Washington, D.C.: National Academy Press, 2000).

16. Ideas similar to the strategy for EU and NATO enlargement advocated in this book have been suggested by others as well. See, for example, Simon Serfaty, "Bigger Is Better," in *Enlargement: A Priority for the European Union,* ed. Christina V. Balis (Washington, D.C.: Center for Strategic and International Studies, May 2001). Serfaty argues that "an implicit strategy of dual enlargement would keep the two processes of enlargement separate, but it would no longer pretend that EU and NATO decisions are separable" (p. 7).

17. See, for example, Goodby, *Europe Undivided,* chap. 5. Greater cooperation was seen within the West, as well as between Russia and the West, than the historical experience would have suggested.

6. An Agenda for a Stable Peace

1. These quotations are from the "Washington Declaration," signed and issued by the heads of state and government participating in the meeting of the North Atlantic Council in Washington, D.C., April 23–24, 1999. Full text at www.nato.int/docu/pr/1999/p99-063e.htm.

2. From the text of the Bush-Putin joint press conference, June 16, 2001, as released by the Office of the Press Secretary, the White House.

3. Address by Prime Minister Guy Verhofstadt at the Seventh European Forum Wachau in Gottweig; online at www.eu2001.be.

4. In a summation of a United States Institute of Peace conference held in Berlin in January 2000 to discuss means of achieving a stable peace in Europe, Stephen Hadley, now U.S. deputy national security adviser to President Bush, advocated "a broader effort by the United States, the European Union, and Russia to develop trilateral cooperation on issues of common concern. A new and affirmative trilateral agenda is required that addresses issues such as nuclear safety, the environment, public health, and rule of law. Dialogue between Europe, Russia, and the United States must begin in earnest." As Hadley also noted, "each leg of the triangle has a unique perspective." He wrote of the U.S. global perspective, the Union's more regional preoccupations, and of Russia as "stuck in a 19th-century realist calculus." In his statement Hadley also wrote that "the United States, the European Union, and Russia can be more effective on certain issues by working together. . . . [E]mphasis should be on patterns of interaction that make practical sense—bringing the right people together to address an issue with approval from senior political levels." We have adopted that approach in our suggestions for trilateral cooperation.

The conference was sponsored by the United States Institute of Peace and the Aspen Institute, Berlin. Hadley and former U.S. national security adviser Anthony Lake participated as cochairs of the United States Institute of Peace's Future of Europe Working Group. The quotation from Hadley is from a United States Institute of Peace Special Report, *Defining the Path to a Peaceful, Undivided, and Democratic Europe* (Washington, D.C.: United States Institute of Peace, June 20, 2000).

5. For an account of one such model, involving the U.S. Joint Strike Fighter, see Greg Schneider, "Allies Enlisted to Pay for Jet," *Washington Post,* March 11, 2001, A1.

6. President Putin has suggested that for at least twenty-five years a U.S. national missile defense program "will not cause any substantial damage to the national security of Russia." See Patrick E. Tyler's report of Putin's meeting with foreign journalists in the Kremlin on June 18, 2001, "Putin Says Russia Would Add Arms to Counter Shield," *New York Times,* June 19, 2001, A1.

7. Putin has proposed that Russian and U.S. intelligence agencies enhance their cooperation to counter illicit trafficking in dangerous technologies. Tyler, "Putin Says Russia Would Add Arms to Counter Shield." President Chirac has proposed an international conference to address ballistic missile proliferation. Our thinking is compatible with these presidential initiatives.

8. Depending on definitions, current U.S. spending on cooperative threat reduction has been between $650 million and $750 million. Thus a 50 percent increase would bring the total to around $1 billion. Compare this with the figure of $3 billion per year recommended in a report submitted in January 2001 by a U.S. Department of Energy task force chaired by former senator Howard Baker and Lloyd Cutler, "A Report Card on the Department of Energy's Nonproliferation Program with Russia," January 10, 2001, available from the U.S. Department of Energy.

9. From the Putin-Bush press conference of June 16, 2001.

10. Sources for the Russian debt picture include Keith Bush, *The Russian Economy in February 2001* (Washington, D.C.: Center for Strategic and International

Studies, 2001); Sabrina Tavernise, "Russia Trying to Head Off Debt Squeeze," *New York Times,* April 14, 2001; and Randall Stone, *Will the West Reduce Russian Debt?* Policy Memo Series no. 195 (Washington, D.C.: Program on New Approaches to Russian Security, Council on Foreign Relations, March 2001).

11. For an excellent discussion of health and foreign policy, see Jordan S. Kassalow, *Why Health Is Important to U.S. Foreign Policy* (New York: Council on Foreign Relations and Milbank Memorial Fund, 2001). The report points out that much higher levels of expenditure will be needed—$30 billion from the international donor community for a global program.

12. An example of a similar program is the effort launched by the Kennan Institute, Washington, D.C., and the Moscow Public Science Foundation to create centers for advanced study and education in three regional Russian universities. This program is being supported by private foundations, in particular, the Carnegie Corporation of New York.

13. Vladimir Putin, acting president of the Russian Federation, "Russia on the Threshold of the Millennium," *Nezavisimaya Gazeta,* December 30, 1999. See also note 1, chapter 2.

14. For an excellent critique of the history of such efforts, see Sarah E. Mendelson and John K. Glenn, *Democracy Assistance and NGO Strategies in Post-Communist Societies,* Working Paper no. 8 (New York: Democracy and Rule of Law Project, Carnegie Endowment for International Peace, February 2000). The study recommended that external assistance be driven more than it is by the local context. Other U.S. scholars have concluded that "the more influence pro-democratic elements in Russia's society have over the development of political institutions, the better the chances that these institutions will become genuinely democratic": Timothy Colton and Michael McFaul, *Are Russians Undemocratic?* Working Paper no. 20 (Washington, D.C.: Russian and Eurasian Program, Carnegie Endowment for International Peace, June 2001).

Index

About the Authors

James E. Goodby is currently senior research fellow at MIT and senior fellow (nonresident) at the Brookings Institution. He has taught at Carnegie Mellon, Stanford, and Georgetown Universities and held the Payne Distinguished Lecturer chair at Stanford during 1996–97. He has written many articles on Europe and Northeast Asia; is the author of *Europe Undivided*, a book on U.S.-Russian relations; and has edited or coedited four other books on U.S.-Russian relations. Entering the U.S. Foreign Service in 1952, he rose to the rank of career minister. His many assignments include deputy to the special advisor to the president and secretary of state for the Comprehensive Test Ban Treaty, 2000–01; special representative of President Clinton for the security and dismantlement of nuclear weapons, 1995–96; chief negotiator for nuclear threat reduction agreements, 1993–94 (the Nunn-Lugar program); head, U.S. delegation, conference on confidence- and security-building measures in Europe, 1983–85; vice chair, U.S. delegation to START I, 1982–83; ambassador to Finland, 1980–81; deputy assistant secretary in the State Department's Bureau of European Affairs and Bureau of Political-Military Affairs, 1974–80; and member, the secretary of state's policy planning staff, 1963–67. He is the winner of the inaugural Heinz Award in Public Policy, the Commander's Cross of the Order of Merit of Germany, and the Presidential Distinguished Service Award. He was named a distinguished fellow of the United States Institute of Peace in 1992. The Stetson University College of Law awarded him an honorary doctor of laws degree in 1996.

Petrus Buwalda was born in the Netherlands and studied at the University of Groningen and at the Institut des Sciences Politiques of the

University of Paris. He entered the Dutch foreign service in 1951 and, after several postings abroad, worked in the directorate for NATO affairs in the Foreign Office in The Hague from 1960 to 1964. After postings as political counselor in Washington and Belgrade he was named deputy permanent representative of his country to NATO in Brussels in 1973. Appointed ambassador to Egypt in 1979, he was named head of the Netherlands delegation to the European Disarmament Conference in Stockholm in 1984 and concurrently served as ambassador to Sweden from 1985. From 1986 to 1990 he was Netherlands ambassador to the Soviet Union in Moscow, representing also the interests of Israel. He ended his diplomatic career as head of the Netherlands delegation to the summit of the Conference on Security and Cooperation in Europe in Paris in November 1990.

Ambassador Buwalda was a visiting scholar at the Woodrow Wilson Center in Washington in 1993. In 1997 the Wilson Center Press published his book, *They Did Not Dwell Alone: Jewish Emigration from the Soviet Union, 1967–1991.*

Dmitri V. Trenin has been deputy director of the Carnegie Endowment's Moscow Center since 1997 and co-chair of its Foreign and Security Policy program since 1994. Until his retirement in 1993 as lieutenant colonel, Trenin served for twenty-one years in the Soviet and Russian Armed Forces. His postings included serving in Iraq with the military assistance group, in East Germany as a liaison officer with the Western allies, in Switzerland with the USSR INF/START delegation, and in Italy as a senior research fellow at the NATO Defense College. He also taught area studies at the current Defense University in Moscow. From 1993 to 1994 Trenin was a visiting professor at the Vrije Universiteit Brussel, and from 1994 to 1997 a senior fellow of the Institute of Europe, Russian Academy of Sciences.

Trenin received his Ph.D. in diplomatic history from the Academy of Sciences' USA-Canada Institute in 1984. His recent publications as author or editor include *The End of Eurasia*; *Russia and the European Security Institutions; Kosovo: International Aspects of the Crisis*; *Russia's China Problem*; *Baltic Chance: The Baltic States, Russia, and the West in the Emerging Greater Europe*; *Commonwealth and Independence in Post-Soviet Eurasia*; and *Russia in the World's Arms Trade*.

Trenin is member of the International Institute for Strategic Studies and of the Russian Association of International Studies. He serves on the editorial boards of *International Politics*, *Pro et Contra*, and *Baltiiski Kurs*.

Yves Pagniez was leader of the French delegation to the Helsinki Summit of the Commission on Security and Cooperation in Europe in 1992. In his distinguished career as a diplomat with the French Foreign Ministry, Ambassador Pagniez served as ambassador of France to the Soviet Union and to the former Yugoslavia. He also served as permanent representative to the United Nations in Geneva and as deputy director for political affairs at the Ministry of Foreign Affairs.

United States Institute of Peace

The United States Institute of Peace is an independent, nonpartisan federal institution created by Congress to promote research, education, and training on the peaceful management and resolution of international conflicts. Established in 1984, the Institute meets its congressional mandate through an array of programs, including research grants, fellowships, professional training, education programs from high school through graduate school, conferences and workshops, library services, and publications. The Institute's Board of Directors is appointed by the President of the United States and confirmed by the Senate.

Chairman of the Board: Chester A. Crocker
Vice Chairman: Seymour Martin Lipset
President: Richard H. Solomon
Executive Vice President: Harriet Hentges

The Association for Diplomatic Studies and Training

The Association for Diplomatic Studies and Training (ADST), a private non-profit organization, advances the study and understanding of American diplomacy and supports the training of foreign affairs personnel at the Department of State's Foreign Service Institute (FSI), which houses ADST's headquarters. Principal ADST activities include the Foreign Affairs Oral History Program, which records and makes available, on CD-ROM and diskette, many hundreds of interviews with diplomatic practitioners; the ADST-DACOR Diplomats and Diplomacy book series; support for FSI training programs, policy seminars, and awards for excellence in language instruction; an ADST research center; and historical exhibits on diplomacy.

A Strategy for Stable Peace

This book is set in Cheltenham; the display type is Cheltenham Bold. The Creative Shop designed the book's cover; Mike Chase designed the interior. Helene Y. Redmond made up the pages. David Compton copyedited the text, which was proofread by Karen Stough. The index was prepared by Sonsie Conroy. The book's editor was Nigel Quinney.